ART
ACTIVITIES
FOR
CHILDREN

ART ACTIVITIES FOR CHILDREN

GEORGE W. HARDIMAN
THEODORE ZERNICH

University of Illinois at Urbana-Champaign

PRENTICE-HALL, INC.
Englewood Cliffs, New Jersey 07632

Library of Congress Cataloging in Publication Data

Hardiman, George W
 Art activities for children.

 Bibliography: p.
 1. Art—Study and teaching (Elementary)
2. Activity programs in
education. I. Zernich, Theodore,
joint author. II. Title.
N350.H27   372.5′044   79-27688
ISBN 0-13-046631-X

© 1981 by Prentice-Hall, Inc., Englewood Cliffs, N.J. 07632

Editorial and production supervision by Hilda Tauber
Cover and interior design by Lee Cohen
Page layout by Judith Matz and Diane Sturm
Manufacturing buyers: Anthony Caruso, Harry P. Baisley

Cover art photography
by W. Duane Powell and Daniel T. Powell

Printed in the United States of America

10 9 8 7 6 5 4 3 2 1

PRENTICE-HALL INTERNATIONAL, INC., *London*
PRENTICE-HALL OF AUSTRALIA PTY. LIMITED, *Sydney*
PRENTICE-HALL OF CANADA, LTD., *Toronto*
PRENTICE-HALL OF INDIA PRIVATE LIMITED, *New Delhi*
PRENTICE-HALL OF JAPAN, INC., *Tokyo*
PRENTICE-HALL OF SOUTHEAST ASIA PTE. LTD., *Singapore*
WHITEHALL BOOKS LIMITED, *Wellington, New Zealand*

CONTENTS

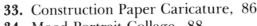

APPENDIX

SUPPLEMENTARY TEACHING AIDS, **135**

INTRODUCTION

This text was written to assist the elementary classroom teacher with little or no training in the visual arts in presenting worthwhile art instruction to children. Implicit is the assumption that no other social institution can provide high quality art experiences for our children as effectively as the schools.

The main themes of this text are that no single rationale for including art in the schools can accommodate the many functions of art, and that the artistic development of children is inextricably mixed with their cognitive development. While enlightened aesthetic perception is the consequence of creating and appreciating art, the most practical entry for elementary students is through creative experience. The activities in this text reflect that orientation.

Part One presents some of the theoretical background necessary to an understanding of how children grow and develop in the visual arts, focusing especially on the concepts of Piaget. Part Two contains 53 graded art activities illustrated by student examples. Supplementary teaching aids can be found in the Appendix.

Art as a Component of General Education

There are numerous reasons for including art instruction in the school curriculum. While arguments for teaching art embody different goals and educational strategies, they all share a deep commitment to a universal art education, and consider art experiences basic to general education.

Although healthy art programs in the schools naturally require advocates among professionals in education, it is reassuring that widespread public support for art instruction also exists. A recent Harris survey documents the considerable grassroots support for improving art instruction in the schools. When questioned about the availability of arts experiences for their children, nearly 80 percent of the respondents felt that schools should make a greater effort in this area. According to this survey, there was strong support for the arts and encouragement for our social institutions to make more quality art experiences available to children. If we examine the nature and function of our social institutions and their potential for effectively delivering art experiences to children, we find that schools have the preeminent responsibility for providing leadership in this area. No other institution in our society is able to systematically handle such a responsibility. Obviously, the elementary school years are crucial to a successful general education, and the visual arts make major contributions to this end.

Before discussing the specific contributions art makes to schooling, it will be helpful to offer a framework for understanding the term general education. According to A.W. Foshay (*Art Education*, 1973), general education includes those domains of knowledge and experience which deal with what it is to be human. He identifies six categories of human development: intellectual, emotional, social, aesthetic, spiritual, and physical. These broad areas of development vary in relevance to the mission of the public schools. For example, schools do not attend directly to social, emotional, and spiritual growth and attend only peripherally to physical development as defined by Foshay. Other social institutions have major responsibilities in these areas. Of these six aspects of general education, the schools make a major and frequently singular contribution to intellectual and aesthetic development. That intellectual development demands over 90 percent of the school week while the arts and other miscellaneous activities account for the remaining 10 percent is disturbing, to say the least. Unquestionably, intellectual development is the work schooling does best. Traditionally, intellectual growth has been limited to skill building in three areas: language arts, computation, and the sciences. In its most responsive sense, the business of the schools should not be restricted to servicing just intellectual development. Rather, the schools should provide the foundation for an understanding of the relationship between the individual and society, and for the preservation and transmission of our common cultural and aesthetic heritage.

Contributions of Art Instruction

INTRINSIC   Art experiences make both intrinsic and extrinsic contributions to the student's general development. Briefly, intrinsic outcomes of art instruction are defined as those outcomes unique to art, and include knowledge about artistic production and perception. The intrinsic view holds that, as a part of the school curriculum, art is an end in itself. This point of view is serviced by learning activities which attempt to build concrete perceptions about the formal and technical properties of art through direct artistic expressions and appreciations. An example of the intrinsic approach can be found in the objectives for the National Assessment Program in Art. These objectives attempted to assess: (a) knowledge about artistic heritage; (b) experience creating works of art; (c) experience perceiving and responding to works of art; and (d) experience justifying judgments about works of art. Intrinsic objectives provide the rationale for much contemporary curriculum development in art, including the lessons in this book.

EXTRINSIC Art instruction can also serve as a catalyst for a number of important extrinsic outcomes in areas other than art. These general extrinsic outcomes tend to transfer readily to human development. Prominent extrinsic outcomes associated with the art experience are encouraging creativity, providing therapy, and promoting leisure time activities.

CREATIVITY

As a creative act, art is seen as an open-ended experience which provides frequent opportunities for imaginative and highly idiosyncratic expression. Research supports the notion that open-ended activities are conducive to creative behavior, particularly activities that value unconventional responses or risk taking with low penalties for failure. Creativity is by no means restricted to art experiences. However, art experiences undoubtedly make significant contributions to creativity in an educational setting.

THERAPY

The therapeutic aspects of art are acknowledged by artists, clinicians, therapists, educators and many others who intuitively feel that art experiences have general cathartic benefits. They support art activities for persons in hospitals, homes for the aged, and the like. According to this point of view, if art is helpful for those with physical, emotional, or behavioral problems, it should have similar benefits for healthy individuals as well.

LEISURE

Futurists often describe a condition where work no longer requires forty hours a week, and thereby provides a much greater opportunity for personal development during leisure time. The argument continues that one important aspect of personal development will be directed toward aesthetic ends, that is, activities organized around artistic involvement. In order to prepare students to take advantage of this opportunity, the basic skills of art production are best acquired in a formal educational setting.

SUMMARY In summary, arguments supportive of extrinsic outcomes are those which see art experiences as fostering broad creative and adjustive behaviors which undergird human development, while arguments supportive of intrinsic outcomes are those which favor specific experiences which are a direct consequence of formal art instruction in the schools. Advocates of both the intrinsic and extrinsic arguments believe that art experiences are basic to an informed general education and that all students should have broad and continuous exposure to art during the elementary and secondary years.

These arguments (see Bibliography for complete references) make a convincing case for art as a basic component of general education. If, as the Harris survey indicates, people believe that art makes a substantial contribution to the general development of their children, there should be little argument about the need to vigorously promote the case for art in the schools just as there can be little argument that a well-rounded, fully integrated general education is the best investment our society can make in its future.

ARTISTIC DEVELOPMENT OF CHILDREN

PART ONE

Understanding how artistic development unfolds during childhood is of central importance to art educators. Researchers tend to agree that children's drawings share certain structural similarities at particular levels of development. In general, there is a scribbling stage (18 months to 3 years); a symbolic stage (3 to 7 years) wherein the fundamental elements of objects are recognizable; and a realism stage (7 years and on) where an effort is made to differentiate forms and details (see Figures 1 to 10). Although some art educators consider the emphasis on stages as too theoretical and inconsistent with the process of individual expression, stages are simply a means by which researchers can begin to describe and organize the cognitive strategies children bring to the act of drawing. As many researchers have demonstrated, the characteristics that define a stage tend to be most representative during the peak period of that stage and not during the beginning or end periods.

PIAGET'S THEORY OF CHILD DEVELOPMENT

Arnheim and Lowenfeld are only two of the many researchers who believe stage theory provides an adequate interpretation of artistic growth. While there is widespread agreement about the classification schemas offered, none effectively ties artistic development to general cognitive growth. Thus, Piaget's theory of cognitive development is attractive to art educators because it has effectively accounted for cognitive differences in the developmental stages of children. There is little doubt that Piaget's theory has particular explanatory inadequacies, but it is commonly agreed that his theory represents the best accounting of cognitive development in children available at this time.

Piaget's work focuses on the qualitative development of intelligence. His research carefully describes and analyzes successive stages of development leading from less to more advanced functional skill. Piaget assumes a qualitative difference, that is, one of kind, between his stages, and not a quantitative difference, that is, one of degree. Because of his qualitative orientation, Piaget believes the human organism tends to organize reality into coherent and stable patterns at certain points of cognitive development which are structurally different and can be analyzed as such. Although Piaget has formally identified three broad stages of human development, much of his writing and the writings of other developmental researchers refer to four broad stages: *sensorimotor,* 0–2 years of age; *preoperational,* 2–7 years; *concrete operations,* 7–11 years; and *formal operations,* 11–15 years. It is important to keep in mind that Piaget's theory is not necessarily determined by age; that is, not all 8-year-olds in all

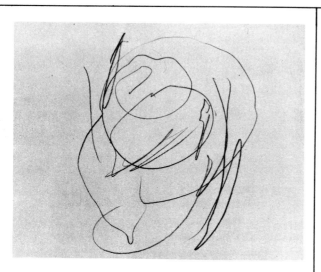

FIGURE 1 *Scribble, preoperational stage, two years old.*

FIGURE 2 *Scribble, preoperational stage, three years old.*

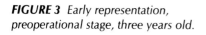

FIGURE 3 *Early representation, preoperational stage, three years old.*

FIGURE 4 *Figure differentiation, preoperational stage, three years old.*

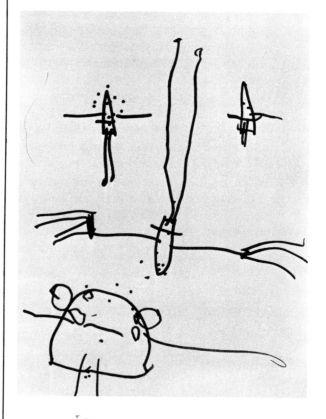

FIGURE 5 *Figural schema,
preoperational stage, four years old.*

FIGURE 6 *Figural schema,
preoperational stage, six years old.*

FIGURE 7 *Figural schema,
concrete operations stage, eight years old.*

FIGURE 8 *Figural schema,
concrete operations stage, nine years old.*

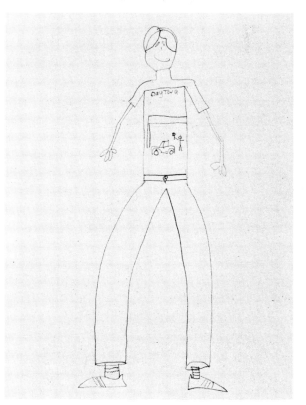

FIGURE 9 *Figural schema, concrete operations stage, ten years old.*

FIGURE 10 *Figural schema, late concrete operations stage, eleven years old.*

cultures can be classified as being in the concrete operational stage. Although there is a positive relationship between age norms and the stages suggested by Piaget across western cultures, there is less similarity across nonwestern cultures. However, although age range and stage are variable across particular nonwestern cultures, from Piaget's point of view all normal children proceed through the same sequence. In short, these qualitative stages emerge in an unchanging order. Stage A always precedes Stage B, but the age at which Stage B appears may vary considerably. In addition, although there are four broad stages, not all individuals need reach mastery or attain the final stage of formal operations, but once a person achieves a higher stage of cognitive development all of the structural properties of the preceding stage become integrated into the stages following.

Before describing those periods of Piaget's developmental sequence that have most application to the drawing development of elementary age children, it will be worthwhile to review his major principles of *equilibrium, structure,* and *schema.*

Equilibrium

The structural properties which define a stage form an integrated whole that Piaget calls equilibrium. This is the major theoretical principle that accounts for the child's transition from one stage to another. Since sta-

4

bility is preferred over instability by all developing organisms, equilibrium is the goal of all organisms. That is, it is inherent in the child's cognitive structure to organize properties into coherent and stable patterns so as to deal effectively with familiar as well as unfamiliar stimuli. Thus, when a new encounter takes place, the child puts it in the context of previous experiences, and using the stability of these previous encounters the child modifies the present perception to respond to the requirements of the new exchange. In terms of drawing development, a schema is an example of a child's cognitive development reaching a level of equilibrium through a particular medium—pencil, crayon, paint, etc. When the child finds that an existing schema does not adequately represent his or her perception of reality, disequilibrium is taking form, such as moving from no baseline to a baseline (see Figure 11). Within the context of Piaget's theory, equilibrium implies a directionality to cognitive development; that is, the child moves from lesser states to greater states of equilibrium which encourage additional understandings of the organism's inconsistencies, and thus, further development.

Advanced stages of development also imply advanced forms of equilibrium. These stages are characterized by the ability to respond to more complicated visual, social, and abstract phenomena, to create more comprehensive classification systems, and to effectively compensate for exchanges with unfamiliar phenomena without greatly influencing the existing states of equilibrium. In short, equilibrium takes the form of increased coherence and stability of integrated cognitive structures. From Piaget's point of view, this increased coherence may be thought of as a complete conceptual attainment, where the individual understands all or most of the important attributes of a conceptual class, knows the rules which define a concept and when to utilize them. For example, a student effectively demonstrates diminution and overlapping of shapes to give the illusion of depth in a drawing (see Figure 12).

FIGURE 11 *Simple baseline organization of shapes.*

FIGURE 12 *Diminution and overlapping of shapes.*

Structure

Most of Piaget's work is directed toward the description and analysis of structural change for all of the broad levels of intellectual development. There are two characteristics of intellectual development: organization and adaptation. Furthermore, adaptation consists of two parts: assimilation and accommodation. Organization is a cognitive necessity since every encounter with our environment involves multiple relations among cognitive actions and the diverse meanings which these actions represent. The adequacy of any perception of any experience depends upon the child's ability to make use of whatever information he or she has, and to build it into a system which correctly interprets the properties of that experience. This is typically accomplished through the general process of adaptation and its subproperties of assimilation and accommodation.

Assimilation means that every cognitive encounter with an environmental object or event involves the cognitive restructuring of the object or event in accord with the child's existing intellectual organization. Accommodation, on the other hand, is the process of adapting oneself to the requirements which are imposed upon the organism. Although Piaget separates the invariant and fundamental properties of assimilation and accommodation for theoretical purposes, in reality they are inseparable and are not observable as separate entities. Therefore, the reason an organism cannot master all that is cognizable in one brief moment is that the organism can only assimilate those things which past assimilations have prepared it to assimilate. In other words, there can never be a radical rupture between the new and the old. Children cannot paint like professional artists because they have not assimilated the prerequisites for behavior at that level of artistic expression.

Schema

Piaget uses the notion of schema in a very general way. He uses it to characterize any generalizable pattern of overt behavior which displays consistency, such as a baby sucking its thumb, grasping behaviors, looking

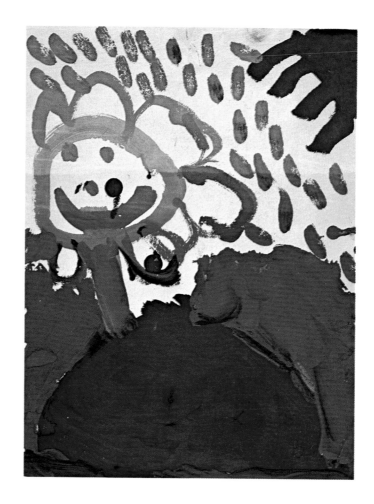

PLATE 1
■ *Spontaneous nonrepresentational use of color.*

PLATE 2
■ *Controlled representational use of color.*

PLATE 3

■ Collage of birds
in their environment (Lesson 3).

PLATE 4

PLATE 5

■ Oil pastel drawing
  of crazy capers (Lesson 4).

PLATE 6

■ *Circus animal marker drawing (Lesson 5).*

PLATE 7

PLATE 8

■ *Oil pastel totem mask (Lesson 6).*

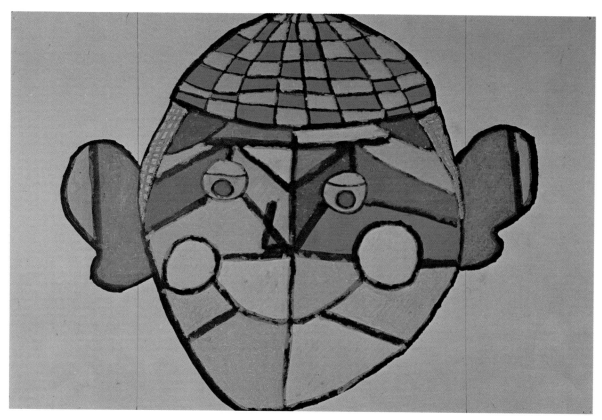

PLATE 9

PLATE 10

■ *Oil pastel drawing of a fantastic garden (Lesson 7).*

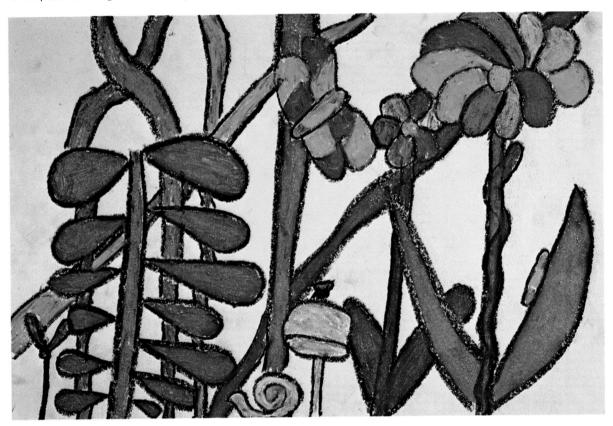

PLATE 11

PLATE 12

■ *Full-body painted portrait (Lesson 8).* **PLATE 13**

■ *Oil pastel story illustration (Lesson 10).*

PLATE 14

PLATE 15

PLATE 16
■ *Drawing of "My family at the kitchen table" (Lesson 11).*

PLATE 17
■ *Scrap stamp print (Lesson 12).*

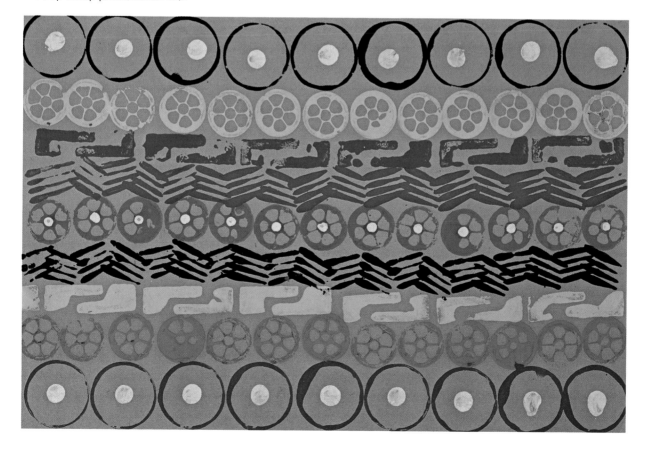

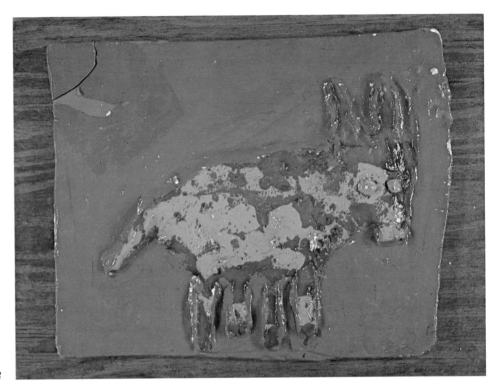

PLATE 18

■ *Clay relief zoo animal (Lesson 14).*

PLATE 19

PLATE 20

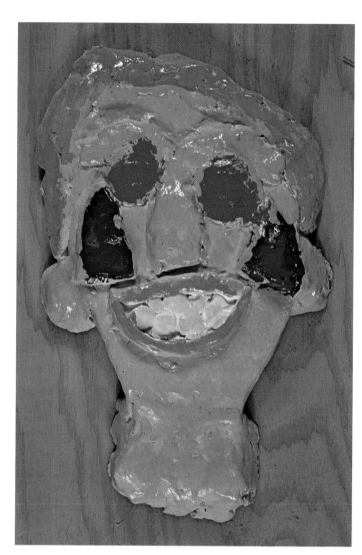

■ *Clay relief portrait (Lesson 15).*

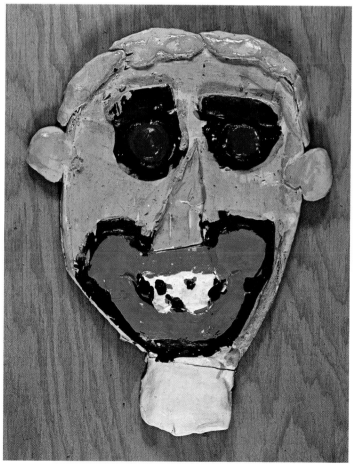

PLATE 21

PLATE 22

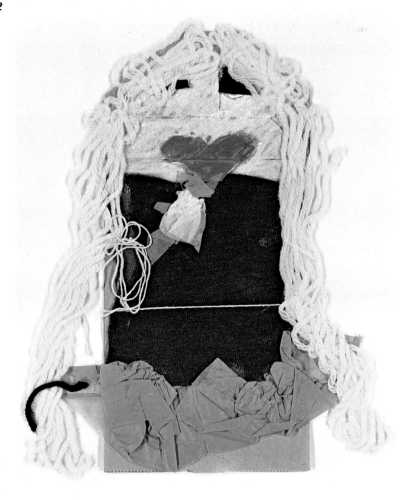

■ *Paper bag puppet (Lesson 16).*

PLATE 23

■ *Tissue paper bird collage (Lesson 18).* **PLATE 24**

■ *Construction paper portrait (Lesson 19).* **PLATE 25**　　　　　　　　　　　　**PLATE 26**

PLATE 27

■ *Oil pastel TIME magazine portrait (Lesson 20).*

PLATE 28

■ *Underwater life or insect tempera batik (Lesson 21).*

PLATE 29

PLATE 30

PLATE 31

■ *Underwater life or insect tempera batik (Lesson 21).*

PLATE 32

behaviors, classification behaviors, and so on. The earliest schemas are relatively simple and tend to be physical in nature while schema found in older children are more complex and tend to be mental in nature. In summary, a schema is an overt form of behavior that is repeatable, consistent, and generalizable to similar classes of behavior.

STAGES OF ELEMENTARY AGE CHILDREN

Although Piaget has identified four broad stages of intellectual development, we will not deal with the sensorimotor stage (birth to 2 years of age) since its application to art instruction appears limited, nor will we deal with the period of formal operations (11–15 years of age) since there is no evidence that children of this period enter an equivalent period of artistic development (Gardner, 1973; Hardiman and Zernich, 1977, 1979; Piaget, 1969). We will focus, instead, on the two stages of development that best characterize elementary age children: (a) preoperational thought (2–7 years of age), and (b) concrete operations (7–11 years of age).

Preoperational Thought

At this point of development, children tend to acquire the capacity to imitate behavior either internally or externally. The internal imitation takes the form of an image, and children use these images as a means for anticipating the outcomes of future actions, such as putting a simple puzzle together. Although the preoperational child can demonstrate transitional problem-solving abilities and is capable of reflecting on behavior as it relates to the accomplishment of some short-term objective, in reality this reflection is faulty by adult standards (Flavell, 1970). The problem is that the preoperational child tends to be egocentric, and hence is unable to see another person's viewpoint, feels no need to justify reasoning, and in general cannot conceive of alternatives to a perceived orientation (Klahr & Wallace, 1970). One of the most observable characteristics of preoperational thought is "centration," that is, the child's tendency to focus on a single feature of an object or event at the expense of other relevant features. The water level problem, where equal amounts of water in identical containers are transferred to containers of different widths and heights and the child is unable to understand that the amount of water has not changed, is an example of the centering problem. The preoperational child is only able to assimilate those features that are most easily perceived.

Preoperational thought is static. It cannot link a set of conditions into an integrated totality; instead, the preoperational child focuses on the individual conditions. Another characteristic of this period is the relative absence of equilibrium. There is no stable and internally consistent cognitive organization with which to order and make coherent the flow of experiences. Thought processes tend to be inflexible, and logical alternatives are not perceived with any consistency. In short, the preoperational stage is a fast-paced period of limited intellectual skills.

Artistic Growth during the Preoperational Stage

Rapid changes in the child's artistic development occur during the pre-operational period. With increasing practice, random scribbles evolve into separate circular enclosures which represent rudimentary human forms. Global circular forms are combined to produce other representational forms. Representational features initially are contained within circular shapes. Gradually, straight line extensions are added to the circular shapes to suggest full frontal figures. As experience with linear media increases, the child's perception and control of other representational features become evident. Simple geometric shapes begin to emerge to represent other facets of the child's immediate environment. Gradually drawings begin to suggest thematic content involving space-time sequences (see Figure 13). While proportional relationships among forms do not typically make themselves evident in the spontaneous drawings done during this stage of development, a simple ordering of shapes does appear in an inconsistent use of baseline or bottom of page spatial organizations.

The following briefly characterizes the preoperational child's orientation to subject matter, color, and space as seen in drawings and paintings.

SUBJECT MATTER

Initially dominated by varieties of human forms, subject matter shapes typically are global circular figures with rudimentary details enclosed. These shapes evolve into more refined circular faces with vertical extensions which gradually are filled in to become static figures in frontal poses. This solution is repeated for all human forms until more details are gradually differentiated. Other familiar kinds of subject matter found in the child's immediate environment, including buildings, animals, and plant life, gradually emerge.

FIGURE 13 Thematic content involving space-time sequences.

COLOR

Initially used spontaneously and nonrepresentationally (see Plate 1), color now is used by the middle and later preoperational child to give subject matter in drawings and paintings a true-to-life or realistic appearance, although there is little apparent concern for control.

SPACE

With practice, random uncontrolled scribbles become separate circular enclosures which take on representational characteristics. Schema for connecting shapes and organizing space gradually appear. Typically no proportional relationships within or among shapes are observed in drawings at this stage.

Concrete Operational Thought

This period is concerned with the intellectual development of middle childhood, 7–11 years of age. At this period Piaget examines the thinking processes which represent a higher degree of logical consistency in handling the mental functions of classification, conservation, egocentrism, and sequencing.

During this period, the child has a coherent and integrative cognitive system which is used to organize and manipulate the immediate environment. The cognitive system has acquired flexibility and consistency. The child has the ability to structure the present in terms of the past without the readily observable contradictions which characterized the previous stage of preoperational thought. As the child progresses through post-infancy, cognitive actions become more and more internalized and form complicated systems of actions, including the ability to organize broad logical actions as well as interpersonal interactions and values. Thus, as the child grows older, attitudes, values, and beliefs begin to stabilize (Kohlberg, 1969). Also during this period the conflicting and often frustrating exchanges with peers create contradictions that may be incompatible. One consequence of these encounters is a definite move away from centration and irreversibility to more complicated forms of thought which are characterized by skills of "decentration" and reversibility (Piaget, 1956).

Clearly, the concrete operational child demonstrates impressive cognitive advancements over the preoperational child. The concrete operations child is in a more advanced state of equilibrium and is therefore better able to organize and stabilize perceptions of the environment. None of these characteristics appear in the behavior of the preoperational child.

Artistic Growth during the Stage of Concrete Operations

The concrete operational child's drawings and paintings become increasingly preoccupied with the realistic representation of familiar objects. As the child gains control of media, drawings become more detailed. Simple proportions can be found within subject matter drawn by the early and middle concrete operational child. Ground line and elevated baseline strategies are frequently used to order and relate subject matter. Rudimentary proportional relationships among objects ordered on top of baselines can be discerned with increasing frequency. Gradually, as the ground line moves up the page and meets the sky to form the horizon, subject matter tends to be drawn within the ground area rather than simply placed on top of the elevated ground line. As the child's natural interest in realistically representing subject matter continues to develop, limited examples of spatial overlap and diminution of size evolve, making a formative attempt to shift from a flat elemental space to a planar space. It should be noted that the child's interest in drawing as a means of describing experiences begins to wane during the later stages of concrete operations, primarily due to the absence of formal art instruction (Gardner, 1977). Because the child does not systematically acquire the essential inventory of art experiences which can be useful in solving simple perceptual inconsistencies that appear in drawings, use of the visual channel of communication atrophies, leaving the more systematically developed verbal channel unchallenged as the dominant mode for qualifying human experience.

SUBJECT MATTER

As might be expected, humans in familiar surroundings continue to dominate the concrete operational child's drawings and paintings. However, unlike the preoperational child's drawing, human figures are less statically depicted and more clearly differentiated in terms of sex and role. Gradually, naturalistic proportional relationships and surface patterns appear and enhance the recognizability of subject matter (see Figure 14). Drawings at the later stage become active, show partial and close-up views, and include both frontal and profile poses of human figures—all of which provide the child a greater opportunity to attend to linear details and proportional relationships. Gradually subject matter may appear in drawings without reference to human figures. Full attention may be given to observing and differentiating interesting compositional arrangements,

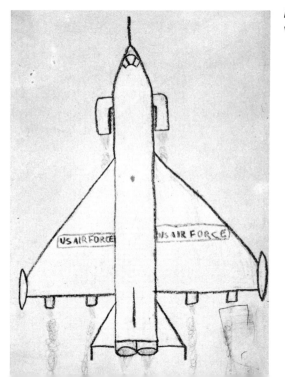

FIGURE 14 *Proportional relationships within subject matter.*

FIGURE 15 *Coordinated spatial organization.*

including plant life, bicycles, room interiors, still life, community buildings, houses, airplanes, cars, animals, and other familiar objects.

COLOR

As was the case for the preoperational child, color is secondary to subject matter in the drawings of the concrete operational child. Flat colors are used to make subject matter appear more realistic. Little color modulation or modelling is used. Better control of media is apparent in the craftsmanship used to color outlined objects (see Plate 2).

SPACE

Early and middle concrete operational children effectively use ground-line and elevated baseline strategies to order and relate the shapes in their drawings and paintings. At this point in development, subject matter is drawn with little apparent concern for proportional differences which exist among various objects. For example, houses may be drawn the same size as humans and trees. As the child's concern for reality increases, proportional relationships gradually emerge, in terms of relationships among objects lined up along a flat baseline (see Figure 15). During this time, uncoordinated spatial organizations juxtaposing baseline views and aerial perspective may appear in drawings. Aspects of elemental perspective as evidenced by diminution of size and spatial overlap may also be seen in the spontaneous drawings of the late concrete operational child. However, it is unlikely that such rudimentary efforts will systematically develop. Unlike their earlier output, at the late concrete operational level children make partial drawings of objects which suggest involvement with objects and actions beyond the immediate picture plane.

To what extent can Piaget's theory provide an explanation of artistic development? Like other theories, his theory represents reality in highly differentiated terms. Although no theory in education and the social sciences has a one-to-one correspondence to reality, theories nevertheless help us to understand how reality may operate. Naturally, there will be examples of children's artistic development that do not correspond to this theoretical orientation, but like all theories that attempt to account for human behavior, these exceptions are within the accepted notions of behavioral probability.

ART
ACTIVITIES

The lessons that follow were carefully selected and field tested for elementary students. They have been taught by both beginning and experienced classroom teachers, and effectively translate art content into successful art activities. There are 53 lessons, grouped into three levels:

Lessons 1 to 16:   Grades 1–2
Lessons 17 to 32:   Grades 3–4
Lessons 33 to 53:   Grades 5–6

Each lesson is a self-contained learning experience for the grade level indicated, but with minor modifications lessons suggested for the lower grades may be effectively taught to older children.

The lessons may be presented in any order. To assist the instructor in making a selection, each of the three groups is preceded by a summary page, listing the lessons under the following areas: collage, drawing and painting, printing, sculpture and construction.

Before presenting a lesson the teacher should review the Materials and the Teacher Preparation sections, and begin collecting the materials for the lesson well in advance. Additional information on supplies, vocabulary, and sources may be found in the Appendix.

Unless otherwise noted, each lesson requires approximately 50 minutes to complete, including motivation, work period, and clean-up. Lessons with multiple sessions are also organized into segments of 50 minutes each. At the conclusion of each lesson the teacher should display all student art work and encourage a class discussion focusing on the subject matter, procedures, and artistic qualities of these objects. Display and subsequent discussion will reinforce the value of these art experiences and provide transitions to the next lesson.

LESSONS
FOR GRADES
 1-2

OIL PASTEL AND PAPER COLLAGE BUTTERFLY

1

MATERIALS
scissors
white glue
pencils
12″ × 18″ black construction paper
12″ × 18″ white drawing paper
oil pastels

PREPARATION
Display photographs of butterflies. Use SVE visuals *Moths and Butterflies* (see Appendix C) if available in your school. If not, *National Geographic, Smithsonian,* and *National Wildlife* are good sources.

It will be helpful to prepare examples of the steps in the procedure: butterfly drawing, butterfly cut into major body parts, colored butterfly, finished butterfly collage.

PROCEDURES
Discuss the shapes and patterns found in photographs of butterflies.

Have students make a line drawing of a butterfly on white paper. Include major pattern shapes in wings and body. Demonstrate how to color pattern shapes by pressing firmly with oil pastels. Direct students to draw and color pattern shapes found in butterfly.

Cut major parts (wings, body, antennae) of colored butterfly into separate pieces. Arrange pieces on black construction paper. *Do not glue.* Have students further cut body parts, this time according to patterns found within each shape, to make a mosaic effect. Each wing and body shape should be separated into at least three shapes.

Reassemble and glue butterfly shapes on black construction paper, leaving about ¼″ space between each colored shape.

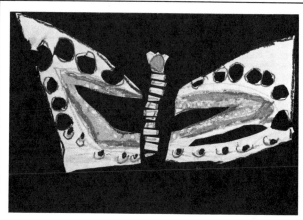

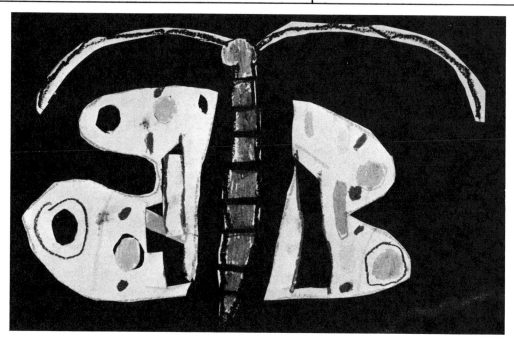

CONSTRUCTION PAPER PORTRAIT: "ME ON TELEVISION"

MATERIALS

pencils
erasers
mirrors
scissors
white glue
12″ × 18″ black construction paper
large scraps white, black, and gray construction paper
small mirrors
transparent tape

TEACHER PREPARATION

Using a piece of 12″ × 18″ black construction paper, cut a shape about the size of a 12″ television screen for each class member.

Collect and display several magazine photographs of frontal portraits (from *Time, Newsweek, Vogue* etc.).

Cut out simplified facial features (eyes, ears, nose, eyebrows, mouth) from black construction paper.

PROCEDURES

Ask students to imagine themselves as television characters. What would they look like? Tape a magazine photograph to paper television screen.

Discuss the shape of the head and facial features.

Tell students that they are to make a self-portrait with all the facial features. Explain that they are to imagine themselves as television characters.

Point out the shapes of facial features in the magazine photographs on display. Ask what shape the head is and where the eyes, nose, and mouth are located. Draw an oval shape on the blackboard to represent a head. Ask for two students to help with the demonstration. Use one student to point out to the class where facial features are located (i.e., eyes approximately in middle of head). Ask other students to tape cut-out facial features to oval shape drawn on blackboard. Discuss location of each feature as student tapes them to the board.

Distribute mirrors. Students should carefully study their own head shapes, before cutting life size head shapes from gray construction paper. Cut and glue head shapes to white television screens. Cut and glue eyes, nose, mouth, eyebrows, hair, and other features from black paper. Glue features to head shapes. When head shapes and features are completed, have students use remaining scraps of paper to make dials and other objects found on front of television sets.

COLLAGE OF BIRDS IN THEIR ENVIRONMENT

MATERIALS
12″ × 18″ manila paper
9″ × 12″ construction paper, assorted colors
scissors
glue

TEACHER PREPARATION
Collect visuals of birds in a setting such as trees, fields, streams, shrubbery, or near residential environments. Visuals which clearly display details of the birds would be most helpful.

PROCEDURES
Discuss various kinds of birds represented in the visuals in terms of color, shape, where they may be found, and different behaviors of birds—flying, nesting, eating, and so forth.

Demonstrate how simple shapes can be used to illustrate the features of birds and their settings.

Demonstrate proper use of scissors and glue.

Tell students that they should cut directly from the 9″×12″ colored construction paper and that there will be no need to draw the shapes first.

Encourage students to fill the entire 12″×18″ manila sheet with birds and the objects found in their setting, that is, trees, shrubbery, water, houses.

Tell students they must use at least four different colors of construction paper.

Encourage students to work neatly.

SEE COLOR PLATES 3 AND 4

OIL PASTEL DRAWING OF CRAZY CAPERS

4

MATERIALS

12″ × 18″ drawing paper
oil pastels
pencils and erasers

TEACHER PREPARATION

On small index cards, write the names of a dozen or more occupations which require the worker to wear a uniform or special outfit, one occupation to a card. Select occupations with which the students are familiar, such as fireman, policeman, nurse, soldier, pilot, dancer, cook, football-baseball-basketball player, doctor, mailman, clown, bus driver, railroad engineer, deep sea diver. Make another set of cards naming several actions and objects of action. Include both realistic actions such as jumping a fence, flying a kite, planting flowers, riding a horse, jumping a rope, playing a violin, etc. and more fanciful actions such as walking an elephant and kissing a lion. Ask students to provide some examples.

PROCEDURES

Ask students to name occupations in which workers wear uniforms or special outfits. Discuss distinctive characteristics of various uniforms. Ask questions about uniform colors, ornamentation, accessories, etc.

Tell students they are going to play a special drawing game where they will be given two cards, one with the name of an occupation like the ones discussed in class and one with the name of an activity. Ask students not to show their cards to their classmates. Students should make a drawing which combines the occupation and the activity (a fireman jumping rope or a nurse walking an elephant).

Demonstrate how to use oil pastels (press evenly to make colors solid). Encourage students to make large shapes, filling the page. When students have finished their drawings, set up a display. Have students guess the occupation and activity depicted by each drawing.

SEE COLOR PLATES 5 AND 6

23

CIRCUS ANIMAL MARKER DRAWING

MATERIALS	pencils and erasers 12″ × 18″ white drawing paper wide felt-tip markers, assorted colors
TEACHER PREPARATION	Have students collect examples of circus animals and bring them to class. Select a circus story and read it to children before beginning the lesson. *The Circus in America* by Charles Fox and Tom Parkinson is a good reference to show children.
PROCEDURES	After reading circus story to class, discuss the different shapes, colors, and sizes of various circus animals. Each student should select a favorite circus animal to draw. Emphasize the importance of a large drawing in order to include relevant details of animals. To insure large drawings, have each animal touch at least three sides of the paper. After completing pencil drawings, students should use felt-tip markers to color the animal.

SEE COLOR PLATES 7 AND 8

25

OIL PASTEL TOTEM MASK

MATERIALS

oil pastels
12″ × 18″ white drawing paper or light-colored construction paper
pencils and erasers
wide black felt-tip markers

TEACHER PREPARATION

With the help of class members collect pictures of masks from different cultures. Old *National Geographic* and *Smithsonian* magazines are useful sources.

PROCEDURES

Use the examples to discuss shapes, patterns, and expressions seen in masks.

Demonstrate how to begin the mask by drawing a large oval face shape with a pencil. Have each student choose an expression his or her mask will demonstrate. Suggest adjectives such as happy, sad, mean, angry, surprised, etc. Draw some shapes on the board. Discuss how mouth, eyes, and eyebrows are shapes for certain expressions.

After the pencil drawings are done, have the students go over the pencil lines with a thick felt-tip marker.

Demonstrate the use of oil pastels. Have students experiment with oil pastels on scrap paper before coloring drawings. Do not cover black marker lines with oil pastels.

NOTE

This lesson may require two sessions to complete careful drawing and coloring.

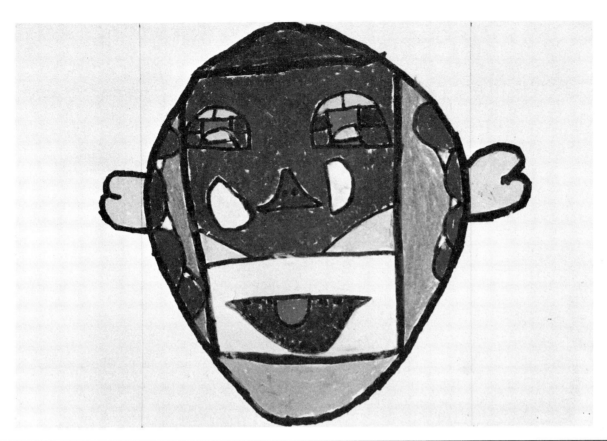

SEE COLOR PLATES 9 AND 10

27

OIL PASTEL DRAWING OF A FANTASTIC GARDEN

1

MATERIALS 12″ × 18″ white drawing paper
oil pastels

TEACHER PREPARATION Collect and display pictures of flowers, insects, and shrubbery commonly found in flower gardens (look in *House and Garden, House Beautiful, National Geographic,* flower catalogs, etc.).

PROCEDURES Have students visualize a one inch tall person walking through a flower garden and how that person would relate in size to the flowers, insects, weeds, rocks, dirt, and other items found there. Discuss what a flower garden would look like from the perspective of a person one inch tall.

Discuss how flowers are different from one another in color, size and shape of petals, leaves, and stems.

Have students begin by drawing outlines of shapes with black lines.

Stress filling the entire page from top to bottom with flower garden shapes. Children should be encouraged to make a dense arrangement of garden shapes. At least half of the total drawing surface should be covered with colored garden shapes.

Demonstrate how to make solid colors by pressing firmly and filling whole shapes with oil pastels.

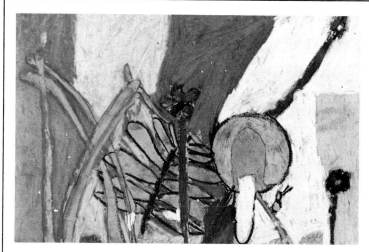

SEE COLOR PLATES 11 AND 12

29

FULL-BODY PAINTED PORTRAIT

MATERIALS 4 ft lengths of brown kraft paper
tempera paints
brushes (large flat and small pointed)
pencils
buckets and sponges
paint containers

TEACHER PREPARATION This lesson will require considerable floor space. Arrange to use gym or an activity room with little furniture.

Set up several painting stations in classroom.

Display magazine pictures of people in motion (participants at sports events, dancers, etc.). Ask students to help collect these several weeks before teaching lesson.

Obtain a record of lively music and record player (optional).

Before second session, pour paint into pint size containers. Each painting station should have one container of each color.

PROCEDURES **Session 1**

Explain to students that they are going to paint a life-size self-portrait.

Discuss relationship of body parts and simple body proportions. Point out waist as middle of body. Compare length of legs to width of shoulders. Estimate how many heads make up body length.

Point out how body parts bend when in motion. Ask for a volunteer. Have the child run in place until you say "freeze." Ask the class to examine how various body parts suggest motion.

With the help of another volunteer, demonstrate the following steps: have the volunteer student lie flat on floor, face up, on top of body-size length of paper; trace outline of student in static position with crayon; have same student lie on a different piece of paper; play record of lively music; ask student to respond by moving arms and legs until you say "freeze"; trace student in active pose; display the two drawings and ask

30

class to compare them in terms of body movement. Tell the class that their full-body portraits have to show similar body movement. Show students how to hold crayon and trace so that body parts are drawn neither too thin nor too thick. Have class pair up and trace each other in active poses with aid of music.

Session 2

Demonstrate how to apply paint to make clothes, face, and other details. Working with their own portraits on the floor, students first should fill in large areas with large brushes. Use small brushes for details only after large areas have dried. Wash the brush each time a new color is used, or paints will get muddy. Colors should be mixed by adding small portions of dark paint to light paint. If one color is to be painted over another, be sure first color is completely dry. Paint should be applied opaquely. When project is finished have students cut out body shapes and assemble them into a class mural.

SEE COLOR PLATE 13

"BRUSHING MY TEETH" MARKER DRAWING

MATERIALS

12″ × 18″ construction paper
thin felt-tip markers
mirrors

TEACHER PREPARATION

Collect pictures of children involved in brushing their teeth. A visit to the dentist or drugstore is a good source for collecting visuals. Ask a few students to bring in a toothbrush for use in a demonstration.

PROCEDURES

Use mirror and other props to perform a skit of brushing your teeth.

Have a volunteer pretend to brush his or her teeth in front of the class.

While the student is demonstrating, point out how the arms bend and how one holds the toothbrush. Discuss what happens to the facial expression, how the mouth opens and teeth become visible.

Discuss what else may be included in the drawing. Have the students name objects found in the bathroom. List these objects on the blackboard.

Distribute materials for drawing. Encourage students to fill entire page with drawing.

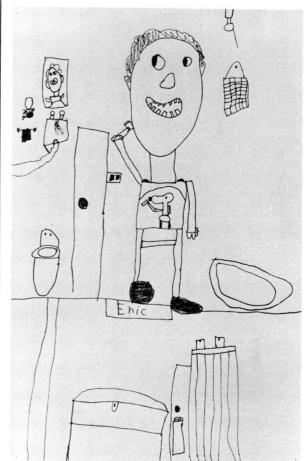

OIL PASTEL
STORY ILLUSTRATION
10

MATERIALS
12″ × 18″ white drawing paper
thin felt-tip markers, assorted colors
oil pastels

TEACHER PREPARATION
Select a short story describing many unusual shapes and figures, and unusual relationships between these shapes (see Notes below).

PROCEDURES
Ask students to respond to the following questions: (1) What is an illustration? (A picture or drawing or diagram.) (2) What is the purpose of an illustration? (It helps to make something like a story clearer, more helpful, or more attractive.) Expand on this idea.

Show some illustrations from storybooks. Ask students what they see in the illustrations and what they think is happening in the story.

Instruct students to listen carefully and pay close attention to the shapes and details described in the story you are going to read. Explain that after the story has been read, students will retell the story by drawing shapes with the markers and later filling in the shapes with oil pastels to make them more solid and colorful.

Emphasize that students should draw as many details as they can remember about the story. Demonstrate use of markers to draw lines. Drawings should be large enough to fill the page. When line drawings are complete, show how to press firmly with oil pastels to make solid color areas.

NOTES
The story you choose to read is important to the success of his lesson. The story must not be lengthy, but must describe many different shapes and unusual relationships between these shapes. A very appropriate story is "The Everlasting Lollipop," about a lollipop that grows bigger every time it is licked, until it grows so big that it must be moved by a crane to the candy store, where an outdoor sign is made of it. Several Dr. Seuss stories also lend themselves to this lesson.

Be sure to read expressively. This will keep the students more attentive to what is going on in the story. They will be eager to illustrate a story they enjoy.

If time permits, have each student discuss his or her drawing before the class.

SEE COLOR PLATES 14 AND 15

35

DRAWING OF "MY FAMILY AT THE KITCHEN TABLE"

MATERIALS
colored markers or oil pastels
12″ × 18″ white drawing paper

TEACHER PREPARATION
With students' help, collect magazine photographs of kitchens and objects found in the kitchen.

Display pictures on bulletin board before teaching lesson.

PROCEDURES
Have students discuss objects found in the kitchen. List on blackboard those objects located on kitchen walls (clock, cabinets, windows, doors, curtains). Make a separate list of objects located on the kitchen floor (sink, counters, tables, chairs, refrigerator, stove).

Tell students they are going to make a drawing of their family sitting at the kitchen table. With help of students, demonstrate how family members can be drawn sitting in both side and frontal views. Encourage students to fill the picture space with kitchen objects. Draw objects located on both walls and floor. Remind students to look at items listed on blackboard to see if they appear in drawing.

Students should first make line drawing with black markers before filling in with colored markers.

NOTE
This lesson is more appropriate for Grade 2.

SEE COLOR PLATE 16

37

SCRAP STAMP PRINT

MATERIALS
wood scraps (squares, circles, triangles, rectangles, odd shapes)
found objects (bottle caps, plastic forks, corrugated cardboard, cups, erasers, etc.)
tempera paint
containers for paint, water
sponges
newspapers
construction paper, assorted colors
brushes

TEACHER PREPARATION
Before teaching this lesson, collect and display examples of simple man-made patterns (wallpaper sample, decorative wrapping paper, clothing, etc.) and natural patterns (flowers, honeycomb, butterflies).

Prepare containers of paint. If available, add a few drops of liquid soap to each pint of paint to aid adherence. You may wish to limit paints to three or four colors.

PROCEDURES
Discuss simple patterns found in examples displayed in class.

Before printing, ask students to point out shapes that exist in the classroom. Explain that an ordered pattern is created when a shape is repeated. An example would be the arrangement of bricks on the classroom wall.

Ask students to point out other ordered patterns in the classroom (clothing, floor tiles, windows). Ask students to point out the man-made or natural patterns which can be seen in the materials collected by the teacher.

Demonstrate how to make a stamp print. Add paint to object's surface with brush. Choose several different shapes from the scrap wood and found object collection you have assembled.

Demonstrate what happens when tempera paint is applied to the surface of an object which is then pressed or stamped onto a piece of paper in an orderly row of shapes. Choose a different scrap shape. Introduce the idea of alternating pattern (for example, stamp a row of circle shapes in

38

one color, then stamp a row of rectangular shapes in a different color—repeat several times).

Demonstrate what shapes various wood scraps and found objects produce when stamped on paper. Ask students to experiment briefly by stamping several shapes on old newspapers. Stamp shapes so they touch each other but do not overlap. The surface should be dense with stamped shapes.

Instruct students to create two finished products. The first can be a randomly stamped experimental print to introduce students to the stamp printing process. The second print should be a simple alternating pattern where the student used several scrap shapes to organize a deliberate pattern.

Situate students in groups of four or five at painting stations.

Each station should have several colors, water, sponges, brushes, and paper towels. The work area should be covered with newspaper.

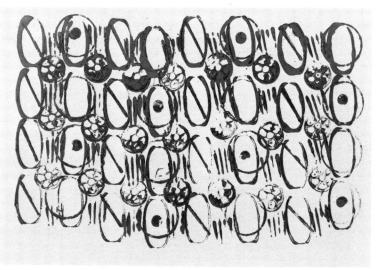

SEE COLOR PLATE 17

STUFFED PAPER BUG SCULPTURE

MATERIALS

36″ × 48″ pieces of brown kraft paper
pencils and erasers
scissors
tempera paints
brushes (large flat and small pointed)
shredded newspaper for stuffing
masking tape
stapler
clothespins or paper clips
polymer gloss medium

TEACHER PREPARATION

Have students help collect colored pictures of insects.

Display pictures of various types of insects before teaching lesson.

Before second session, set up several painting stations, prepare containers of paint, collect and shred newspapers.

PROCEDURES

Session 1

Lead a discussion on different types of insects. List on the blackboard those that crawl and those that fly.

While examining pictures, discuss and compare shapes of body segments, legs, wings, heads, and antennae.

Explain how insects' bodies often have patterns, or a repeated arrangement of lines and shapes.

Have students point out patterns in their own clothes and in the room. Find patterns in pictures of insects, isolating the kinds of shapes, lines, or colors that make up the patterns.

Demonstrate procedure for making paper bug. Fold 36″ × 48″ piece of brown paper in half and draw insect large enough to touch all four edges of folded paper. Draw details and patterns on one side of the bug.

Session 2

Paint both sides of bug with tempera paints.

Cut out insect shape and staple together about two-thirds of the way around. Loosely stuff with shredded newspaper and staple the rest. Cover finished insect with a coat of polymer gloss medium. Each student should select an insect to draw and consider its particular body shape and patterns.

Wash brushes each time a new color is used. Colors should be mixed by adding small portions of dark paint to light paint.

NOTES   If the two sides of the bug do not fit properly, trim the excess paper. Be careful not to overstuff, so the paper will not crack. With the help of teacher aid, paint finished insect with a coat of polymer gloss medium.

This project may require more than two sessions to complete.

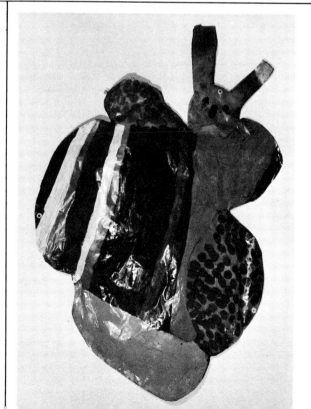

CLAY RELIEF ZOO ANIMAL
14

MATERIALS balls of clay (grapefruit size), 1 for each student
plastic knives and forks for cutting and scoring clay
water buckets, sponges
plastic bags
tempera paints
polymer gloss medium
brushes
10 × 10″ cardboards for storing reliefs
wood squares for mounting finished products (optional)

TEACHER PREPARATION Collect and exhibit photographs of various animals. Choose simple side views which reveal the complete animal shape.

Make examples of the project to show students.

Prepare ball of clay for each student.

PROCEDURES **Session 1**

Explain the animal clay relief project briefly, showing example of an animal you have done. The first session will involve making the basic shape of the animal; the second session will be used to paint the animal with tempera.

Examine the visual aids while discussing the basic shape and size differences among animals. Point out how much longer the neck of a giraffe is in comparison to the legs. Have students describe basic shapes found in other animal pictures.

Show how to make the animal relief. After covering work surface with plastic bag, use approximately one-half the ball of clay to make a flat clay slab about one-half inch thick. Explain that a clay relief which is too thick may crack. Demonstrate how to draw side views of animals on the slab and cut out. Scraps of clay should be balled up to keep moist.

Explain texture as the way the surface of an object feels, for example, smooth or rough (see Appendix B for other descriptive terms). Talk about different animal textures. Demonstrate how to make different types of textures and attach them to the clay slab animals. Show how to make coils. Show how to curl the coils as well as use them straight.

Distribute materials and have students make clay reliefs of their favorite zoo animal. When finished, place on 10 × 10″ cardboard with student's name clearly written on masking tape and affixed to corner. Loosely cover with plastic and store.

When relief plaques are thoroughly dry in about one or two weeks, fire them in a kiln to 1500°F.

Session 2

In preparation for painting, teacher should briefly soak the fired animal reliefs in water to lessen absorbancy. Demonstrate how to coat the animals with a base layer of white paint. Cover all cracks and edges so no raw clay shows. When dry, paint in desired colors. If you wish, reliefs may be sealed with a coat of polymer gloss medium.

Reliefs may then be mounted on a painted wooden plaque and framed for display. Use epoxy glue to mount.

SEE COLOR PLATES 18 AND 19

CLAY RELIEF PORTRAIT

MATERIALS

balls of clay (grapefruit size), 1 for each student
knives and forks for cutting and scoring clay
plastic bags (small and large)
wood squares for mounting finished portraits
water buckets, sponges
polymer gloss medium
tempera paints
brushes (large flat bristle brushes and small pointed brushes)

TEACHER PREPARATION

At least one week prior to teaching the lesson, ask children to bring covers from *Time, Newsweek,* and other magazines which feature portraits on the cover.

Display reproductions and pictures of the frontal face.

Make a completed slab relief portrait to show children.

Prepare ball of clay for each student.

Before the second session, pour paints into containers. Each painting station should have one container of each color.

PROCEDURES

Session 1

Have students respond to the following questions: How do we all recognize each other? What shapes are people's heads? Are they round, oval, square, diamond? Point to visuals and students' heads as examples. What parts of the face are most noticeable and how are they shaped (mouth, nose, eyes, ears, eyebrows, hair, cheeks, chin, etc.)? Again refer to the visuals and students' faces as examples. These features may be reduced to basic shapes (*mouth:* diamond, half moons, circle, rectangle; *eyes:* round, almond, oval; *nose:* round, rectangle, triangle; *eyebrows:* rectangle, triangle, half moons, almonds; *ears:* semi-circles *hair:* coils, circles, cylinders).

Cover work surface with plastic bag. Using approximately half the ball of clay, demonstrate how to flatten it with the hands into a slab no thinner than one-half inch. From it cut out an oval head shape. Show example of completed slab relief face, and briefly explain simple ideas of proportion and placement, referring to visuals and real human faces. Dem-

44

onstrate how to make and attach facial shapes from rest of clay by coiling, cutting, shaping, scoring, and pressing into slab.

To store, wrap loosely in plastic. For easier handling, put slabs on pieces of scrap wood or cardboard approximately 10 × 10″ with student's name clearly written on masking tape and affixed to corner.

Allow completed face to dry slowly but thoroughly, about one to two weeks. Slow fire in kiln to 1500°F.

Session 2

You may want to set up several painting stations in the classroom with water buckets and clean-up materials at each station.

Before painting the fired clay faces, the teacher should briefly soak them in water so they do not absorb too much paint.

Explain how the clay faces have been fired in the kiln and are now ready to be painted. If any pieces have fallen off, they can be glued on again with epoxy glue after painting.

First, paint a background color or base coat. Using a wide brush, cover the entire face evenly with a light color of paint. Demonstrate how every crack and hole and edge must be painted, so none of the raw clay color shows through. Do not paint too thickly, or base coat won't dry in time to add the features.

After base coat is completely dry, demonstrate how to paint features and details with a small brush. Stress neatness and careful painting.

NOTES This project will require at least two sessions to complete. Reliefs may be sealed with a coat of polymer gloss medium and mounted on a painted wooden plaque.

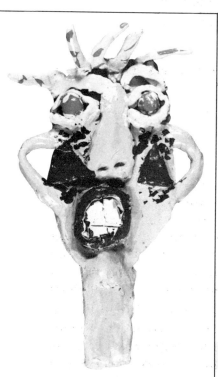

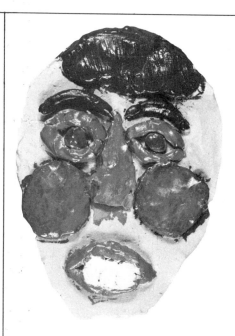

SEE COLOR PLATES 20 AND 21

45

PAPER BAG PUPPET

MATERIALS

paper lunch bags
12″ × 18″ construction paper, assorted colors
scissors
glue
yarn
oil pastels

TEACHER PREPARATION

Make example of finished paper bag puppet before teaching lesson.

PROCEDURES

Discuss the shape of various facial features and how combinations of these features produce different looking faces. See Lesson 15 for details.

Demonstrate how features are drawn on construction paper and glued to paper bag: The mouth is glued under the flap of the bag, the eyes and nose are glued on top of the flap, and ears are attached to the sides or tops. Yarn or similar material can be used for hair.

Demonstrate how the hand can manipulate the flap of the puppet bag to simulate talking.

Students may perform short skits with the puppet bag characters.

NOTE

Lesson should be taught at second grade.

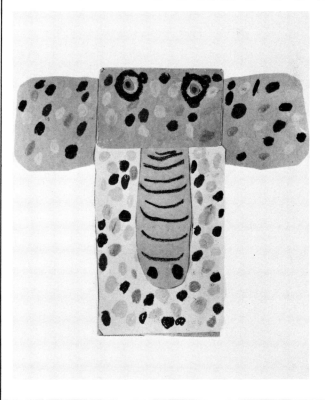

SEE COLOR PLATES 22 AND 23

47

LESSONS FOR GRADES  3-4

CONSTRUCTION PAPER BIRD

MATERIALS
scissors
9″ × 12″ construction paper, assorted colors
construction paper scraps, assorted colors
white glue
pencils

TEACHER PREPARATION
Display photographs of common birds.

Cut enough construction paper in half (6″ × 9″) so every student gets two half sheets.

PROCEDURES
While examining photographs, discuss differences among birds—in sizes, shapes, and colors of bodies, tails, wings, feathers, necks, beaks, feet, etc. Instruct students to choose one 9″ × 12″ sheet of construction paper and two 6″ × 9″ sheets in another color.

Draw and cut out the body shape of a bird from one 6″ × 9″ piece of paper. The body shape should be big enough to touch all four edges of the 6″ × 9″ sheet.

After examining different wing shapes, cut out wings from the other 6″ × 9″ paper, and glue body and wings into position on 9″ × 12″ construction paper.

Students may cover birds with feathers several ways: by tearing pieces of paper, by cutting and fringing edges, or by cutting strips and curling ends. Irregular sizes of feathers can be very interesting, so do not worry about making feathers uniform in size. Select two or three colors from scraps of paper for feathers. Attach them to the bird body with white glue. Encourage students to use imaginations to create unique and exciting new birds.

After applying feathers, add eyes, beak, legs, and feet, using remaining paper scraps.

NOTE
This lesson may take more than one session to complete.

TISSUE PAPER COLLAGE

MATERIALS

pencils and erasers
12″ × 18″ white drawing paper
everyday objects (scissors, stapler, pencil sharpener, lightbulb, etc.)
wide black felt-tip markers, waterproof
diluted white glue (1 part glue to 2 parts water)
brushes (1″ wide)
scissors
tissue paper, assorted colors
construction paper, assorted colors

TEACHER PREPARATION

Have students collect pictures of common birds.

If available in your schools, display SVE visuals of familiar birds (see Appendix C). Set up display before teaching lesson.

Obtain a copy of "The Ice Cream Cone Coot" by Arnold Lobel.

PROCEDURES

Students are to make unusual birds from drawings of everyday objects.

Ask students to name several things all birds have in common and list these on the chalkboard (wings, beak, feathers, claws, tail, etc.).

Discuss how birds are made from everyday objects in "The Ice Cream Cone Coot." It may be helpful to make another list of objects suitable for transformation into birds.

Demonstrate the steps involved: First, lightly draw the contours of an everyday object in pencil. Add common bird features using simple, basic shapes such as circles and triangles.

Complete the pencil drawing, adding details such as feathers. Trace over the pencil drawing with the waterproof marker to make the lines thick and dark.

Add tissue paper. Demonstrate how to use glue mixture and brush. Apply glue under and over torn or cut tissue paper pieces. Glue down corners of paper. It does not matter if the tissue paper overlaps the outside lines since the drawing eventually will be cut out. Do not use too much glue.

Show how the paper can be cut or torn to fill different areas such as the head, beak, eyes, and wings.

Since much of the tissue paper will be dark, show how to achieve lighter colors in certain areas (like a robin's underside) by overlaying light tissue.

Show how paper can be crumpled to create rough texture effect for parts like tail feathers and wings.

After glue is dry, retrace lines with black marker to make them dark and visible. Students may cut out finished birds and mount them on colored construction paper.

NOTE   This lesson will take at least two sessions to complete.

SEE COLOR PLATE 24

CONSTRUCTION PAPER PORTRAIT

MATERIALS small mirrors
scissors
glue
erasers
12″ × 18″ construction paper, assorted colors

TEACHER PREPARATION With help of students, collect and display examples of portraits from magazines (*Time, Vogue, Newsweek*).

PROCEDURES Define *self-portrait* as usually a drawing or painting of an artist made by the artist. Tell students that they are going to make a different kind of self-portrait by cutting and tearing construction paper.

Discuss magazine portraits by asking questions about the shape and size of eyes, nose, mouth. Using a student as a model, point out the relative placement of facial features—eyes in middle of head, nose at midpoint between eyes and mouth. Compare the size of the end of the nose with an eye. Then compare with magazine portraits on display.

First cut an oval head shape and a neck and shirt shape. Demonstrate how to cut the eyes, ears, nose, mouth, eyelashes, teeth, and other facial details from construction paper. Demonstrate how to tear paper to suggest hair. Ask children for advice about where to place features. Compare placement with examples from magazine pictures.

Finished portrait should fill most of the 12″ × 18″ construction paper.

SEE COLOR PLATES 25 AND 26

OIL PASTEL "TIME" MAGAZINE PORTRAIT

MATERIALS

9" × 12" white drawing paper
pencils
erasers
oil pastels
hand mirrors
scissors
9" × 12" red construction paper
white glue
white or yellow paper scraps

TEACHER PREPARATION

At least one week before teaching lesson, ask students to collect covers from *Time, Newsweek, Vogue,* and other magazines which feature frontal portraits on cover.

Set up display of portraits of magazine covers along with examples of frontal portraits done by artists.

Prepare examples of various stages: pencil drawing, partially colored portrait, and finished portrait.

PROCEDURES

Session 1

Define *self-portrait* (drawing or painting of artist made by the artist). Show examples of artists' portraits. Describe facial construction, using student as model. Discuss the relative placement and size of eyes, ears, nose, and mouth; have students analyze and compare the organization of facial features in the magazine covers and reproductions.

Distribute hand mirrors and ask students to study their facial features.

Have students make a light contour line drawing of frontal self-portraits on white drawing paper. (A contour line drawing follows the outside edges, or contours, of shapes.) Paper should be used vertically. Stress the importance of careful observation of facial details and proportions. Ask students to compare the placement of features in their drawings with the magazine covers and reproductions.

Session 2

Demonstrate how to use oil pastels. Colors applied to drawings should be solid and bright.

Fill in colors over pencil drawings, then cut out portraits and glue them on red 9″ × 12″ construction paper.

Reproduce *Time* logo with cut paper letters, and glue it above portraits at the top of the red construction paper.

SEE COLOR PLATES 27 AND 28

UNDERWATER LIFE OR INSECT TEMPERA BATIK

MATERIALS

12″ × 18″ construction paper
white chalk
paint brushes (½″ pointed and 1″ flat bristle)
permanent black ink
tempera paint, assorted colors
containers for paints, ink, and water
newspapers

TEACHER PREPARATION

Collect reproductions illustrating fish or insects in their natural habitat. SVE visuals are excellent for this purpose (see Appendix C).

It would be helpful to have on hand examples òf various stages of this project: a chalk line drawing and a painted picture ready to be covered with ink.

PROCEDURES

Session 1

Discuss the kinds of lines, shapes, patterns, and colors typically found in underwater life. Refer to examples of underwater life offered by reproductions. Have students use chalk to draw outlines of underwater or insect subject matter in environment. Simplified surface patterns found in underwater and insect subject matter should be carefully observed and drawn with chalk.

Session 2

Demonstrate how tempera paint is applied within shapes and not over the chalk lines. Unpainted space should be on either side of chalk lines. Tempera paint should be applied thickly. Spaces not covered with chalk or tempera paint will be black in final product.

Once tempera paint is thoroughly dry, cover entire sheet with an even coat of permanent black ink. Set aside to dry.

Session 3

When ink is dry, teacher or teacher aid should immerse entire work under faucet and remove ink from tempera paint by gently rubbing with bristle brush. A certain amount of ink should be retained to create batik effect.

NOTE The success of this project depends on the care taken when removing ink from the tempera surface. Since the paper can easily tear at this stage, Session 3 should be done by teacher or teacher aid at this grade level.

SEE COLOR PLATES 29–32

SEA LIFE OIL PASTEL RESIST

MATERIALS 12″ × 18″ light-colored construction paper
pencils
oil pastels
black tempera paint
brushes (1″ flat bristle)
containers for water and paint

TEACHER PREPARATION Collect reproductions illustrating fish in their natural habitat.

PROCEDURES Point out patterns and colors of fish seen in photographs.

Demonstrate steps involved in the process of oil pastel resist: Draw outline of an underwater sea life scene in pencil; color in the drawn shapes with bright oil pastel color; paint over the picture with a black tempera paint; rub off excess paint with sponge.

Stress that in drawing and coloring, some empty spaces should be left between colored areas so black paint will show. Stress that oil pastels must be applied with firm pressure to resist paint. Demonstrate how to use oil pastels. Avoid using black oil pastel since it will not show.

NOTE This lesson may take two sessions to complete.

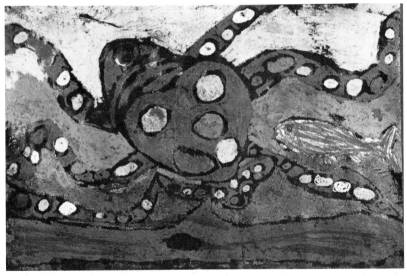

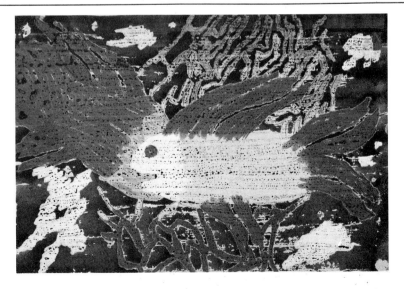

SEE COLOR PLATE 33

"WANTED" POSTER PORTRAITS

MATERIALS
12″ × 18″ white drawing paper
pencils and erasers
colored felt-tip markers of oil pastels

TEACHER PREPARATION
With the help of students, collect and display magazine photographs of frontal and side poses of heads.

Write names of students in class on slips of paper.

PROCEDURES
Ask students to describe what a "wanted" poster might look like. Ask students why wanted posters try to show both frontal and side views of the head. Discuss how side view of head differs from frontal view. Referring to magazine photographs, point out differences in head shapes, eyes, hair, ears, noses, mouths, necks, foreheads, chins, etc.

Tell students that they are going to make special wanted posters of other members of the class. Names will be drawn from a hat. Children should make both frontal and side view drawings of the name drawn from hat. Drawing paper should be divided into two 9″ × 12″ sections. Outlines of each pose should be drawn with black marker or oil pastel. Drawings should fill the space. As many details as possible should be included for each pose. Colors should be added when all features have been drawn.

When drawings are finished, encourage students to add other information found on wanted posters, such as description of offender (height, weight, age), description of offense, reward. Ask students to make up some *good* deeds that the class member might be wanted for, such as helping a friend with homework or taking out the garbage.

Wanted!
Nasty Knuckles
For Hitting Old Laddies on The Street BEWARE!!!
Dead or Alive
Front View

Wanted;
Nasty Knuckles
For Hitting Old Laddies on The Street BEWARE!!!
Dead or Alive
Side View

happy   front-veiw

WANTED: THE JOKER
for Smiling too much
DEAD or Alive
But would like it more if he was brougt in dead!

Dead   side-veiw

WANTED: THE JOKER
for Smiling to much
DEAD or ALive! But would prefer him Dead!

63

TAGBOARD RELIEF PRINT OF FANTASY CREATURE

MATERIALS

tagboard (old manila folders)
carbon paper
white glue
scissors
inking plates (glass or plexiglass)
brayers for rolling ink
black water-base ink
colored tissue paper, assorted colors
12″ × 12″ newsprint

TEACHER PREPARATION

With help of children, librarian, and perhaps a high school science teacher, collect and display pictures of a variety of insects (bird's-eye views are most revealing of exterior shapes and body markings).

Before Session 3, set up a printing station to accommodate no more than four to five students at one time.

PROCEDURES

Session 1

Discuss insect characteristics evident in photographs. Particularly note the exterior shapes, number of legs, size of legs, other features and surface patterns of body markings. Define *pattern* as an organized arrangement of repeated lines, circles, and other shapes to create a design on the insect's body. Students will combine different insect characteristics to create an unusual insect of their own making.

Ask students to take the features from two or three different insects (legs from grasshopper, body of beetle, wing markings of butterfly) and combine them into one fantasy creature. Demonstrate how to first draw the exterior body shapes in contour line on 12″ × 12″ newsprint, then add body markings or patterns. Fill entire 12″ × 12″ page with insect shape.

When finished, show how to use carbon paper to transfer drawing onto tagboard. Trace only the body outline.

Session 2

Demonstrate how to cut solid body shape neatly from tagboard and glue onto cardboard surface. Cut out other parts (legs, head, and antennae) from tagboard and glue down, leaving ¼ inch between each shape. In the final print, the spaces will appear as white lines separating the various body parts. Cut and glue markings and patterns (stripes, dots, combinations) over body of insect.

Session 3

Printing should be done by no more than four or five students at one time. Squeeze out one inch of ink onto inking plate. Roll brayer over glass plate vertically and horizontally to spread ink evenly.

Roll inked brayer over cardboard plate vertically and horizontally for even transfer of ink. Lay tissue paper over inked cardboard plate and rub evenly with heel of hand or clean brayer. When ink is evenly transferred, pull print and set aside to dry. Encourage students to print papers of different colors.

SEE COLOR PLATES 34 AND 35

CARICATURE STRING PRINT

MATERIALS

9″ × 12″ noncorrugated cardboard (gift boxes)
pencils and erasers
drawing paper
carbon paper
2-ply string
white glue
scissors
small mirrors
black water-base printing ink
brayers
inking plates (glass or plexiglass)
colored tissue paper or construction paper

TEACHER PREPARATION

Collect and display caricatures and photographs of politicians, movie stars, and sports figures. Photographs and caricatures of the same person will permit comparisons between photographic representation and caricature.

PROCEDURES

Session 1

Explain the meaning of caricature. Using a photo and caricature of the same person, ask students what feature or features the artist has exaggerated to make the caricature. Why were those features exaggerated? Discuss how to select a feature for exaggeration.

Start self-caricatures by lightly drawing the face shape and facial details. Students should use mirrors and be instructed to pay careful attention to facial proportions and details. When students have finished initial drawing they should exaggerate the one facial feature which they feel best characterizes them by drawing it larger than life.

Session 2

Transfer caricatures onto matboard or cardboard with carbon paper.

Demonstrate how to glue string over lines drawn on the matboard plate. Remove excess glue. Emphasize neatness.

Session 3

When glue is completely dry, demonstrate how to ink the glass plate with brayer moving horizontally and vertically, how to evenly transfer the ink to the string plate with brayer, then print on tissue paper or construction paper. (See Lesson 44 for more complete instructions on the printing process.)

NOTES   Encourage students to break up large areas with string and glue to achieve a good quality print. If large areas are not broken up, ink will get into those areas and print. Explain that you want only the string to print.

GLUE LINE RELIEF PRINT

MATERIALS
pencils and erasers
white glue
noncorrugated cardboard 11″ × 14″ or smaller
inking plates (glass or plexiglass)
brayers
water-base printing inks, assorted colors
18″ × 24″ newsprint paper
tissue paper, assorted colors
construction paper, assorted colors

TEACHER PREPARATION
Collect and display pictures of insects, animals, vehicles, horses, and other subject matter.

Make example of glue line plate to show students.

PROCEDURES

Session 1

Have students make a contour line drawing of their subject matter directly on cardboard plate. Stress careful observation of details. Object should cover the 11″ × 14″ surface. Environmental shapes can also be included but should be minimized.

Session 2

Briefly describe the glue line relief process using samples from the various steps. Show how to apply glue lines over the pencil lines to create about ⅛″ relief. Avoid putting glue lines too close together, so as not to trap globs of ink. Take care not to smudge the wet glue. When finished, place wet glue plates on a flat surface to dry.

Session 3

Explain how in positive relief printing, printed design is taken from what is applied or raised on the surface of the cardboard plate. In this case, glue has become the raised surface on the plate. Ink is spread evenly onto inking plate with brayer, rolled horizontally and vertically, then transferred with the brayer to the plate so that ink adheres to the raised glue surfaces and onto some of the background, leaving an uninked area surrounding the edges of the image which will not print. Stress that the plate must be completely and evenly inked. After inking, move plate to a clean place.

Prints are made on construction or tissue paper by rubbing with a clean brayer, cylindrical object, or even the heel of the hand. Check the progress of the transfer by picking up the corners of the print. Set print aside to dry when ink is evenly transferred. Caution: Water-base ink dries quickly, causing paper to stick to plate if delay occurs between inking the plate and making the print.

NOTES Have newsprint on hand for practice before using the good tissue paper. Practice prints are called proofs.

Encourage neatness, and stress that it is important to keep hands and area around paper clean during the whole process of printing.

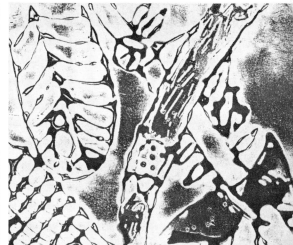

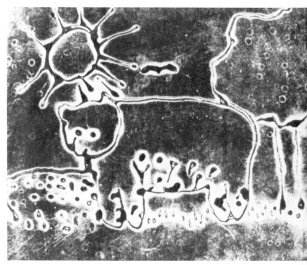

FANTASY CREATURE BOX SCULPTURE

MATERIALS found objects (small boxes, cardboard tubes, egg containers,
  milk cartons, bottle caps, spools, wood scraps, straws, Q-tips, etc.)
construction paper scraps
scissors
glue
tempera paint
brushes (1″ flat bristle and small pointed brushes)

TEACHER PREPARATION With the help of children, collect an assortment of found objects such as those listed above.

Collect and display illustrations of animals.

PROCEDURES Discuss the general shape of an animal and demonstrate how to construct basic animal shape. Show how found objects can be combined and attached to form fantasy creatures. Stress careful attachment and gluing of parts.

After the basic animal form is completed, show how to embellish by attaching bottle caps, spools, wood chips, etc. to depict facial features, hoofs, tails, and other details. Construction paper scraps can be shaped into small tubes, curled, folded, or scored to create surface textures.

The following materials are suitable for body detail and texture: *eyes*—bottle caps, styrofoam pieces; *nose*—cardboard tubing, small boxes, wood; *mouth*—boxes cut in half, cardboard tubing; *teeth*—wood, styrofoam, construction paper; *horns, ears*—cups, tubing, wood; *tails*—tubing, cups, styrofoam, small boxes; *legs, feet, hoofs*—tubing, small boxes.

When construction is finished, the sculptures can be painted white, then decorated with other colors.

NOTE Plan on using three sessions for this lesson.

70

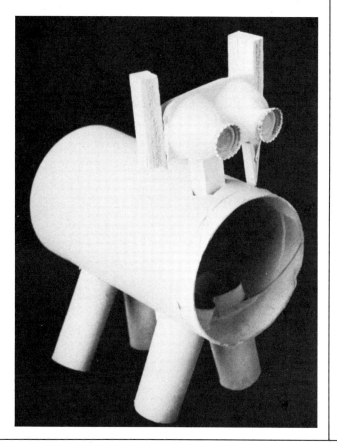

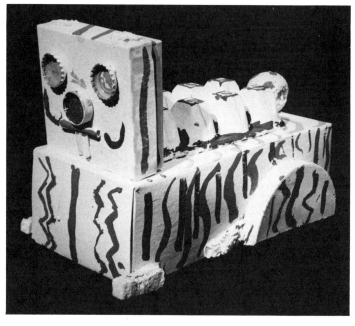

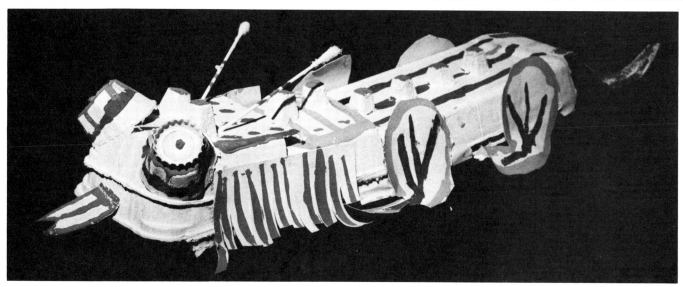

SEE COLOR PLATES 36 AND 37

CLAY RELIEF HOUSE

MATERIALS
balls of clay (grapefruit size), 1 for each student
pencils and erasers
rulers
9″ × 12″ drawing paper
clay tools, including knives and forks
water buckets, sponges
plastic bags
brushes (1″ flat bristle and small pointed brushes)
tempera paint
pieces of 10 × 10″ cardboard for storing reliefs
polymer gloss medium
wood squares for mounting plaques (optional)

TEACHER PREPARATION
Ask students to collect pictures of houses from magazines. Ask a local architect for old copies of professional magazines. A few days before teaching the lesson, display pictures prominently in classroom.

Prepare ball of clay for each student.

PROCEDURES

Session 1

Ask students to think about the frontal appearance of their own houses. Motivate them with questions about the size, number, shape, and location of doors, windows, and other features. Consider roofs, porches, chimneys, steps, etc.

Explain idea of overlapping shapes—how, for example, a bush may hide part of the house behind it. Find overlapping shrubs and other shapes in photographs. Look also at the relative sizes of objects, such as the size of trees compared to houses.

Instruct students to make drawings of the front of their own house. Drawings should be no larger than 9″ × 9″. The house shape should dominate the page, although trees, shrubs, porches, and other nearby things may be included.

Session 2

Explain to students that they are going to make a clay relief of their house.

Working on plastic, demonstrate how to make two 9″ square slabs ½″ thick out of halves of clay ball. Using the drawings done during Session 1, trace house shape and details on clay slab and cut out. Show how to make two pieces of clay adhere to each other by scoring (roughing the surfaces to be joined with a fork). Use clay slab scraps to cut out windows, doors, shingles, siding, and other details included in the drawing and attach them to house slab. Students should place their initials on back when finished. Cover loosely with plastic for slow drying. Let dry on cardboard to keep flat. When reliefs are thoroughly dry (about two weeks), fire slowly in kiln to 1500°F.

Session 3

Before painting, have students soak plaques briefly in water to decrease absorbancy. Demonstrate how to cover the entire surface with a base layer of white tempera paint. Paint inside cracks and along plaque sides too. After base coat is dry, paint reliefs with bright colors. For protective finish, brush on a layer of polymer gloss medium after tempera paint is completely dry.

Reliefs may be mounted on wood squares (¼″ plywood) with epoxy glue.

SEE COLOR PLATE 38

CLAY RELIEF JUNGLE FOLIAGE

MATERIALS

balls of clay (grapefruit size), 1 for each student
pencils and erasers
9" × 12" drawing paper
wood squares for mounting finished product
newspaper for clay working surface
clay tools for cutting and scoring
water buckets, sponges
large plastic bags
tempera paints
brushes (1" flat bristle and small pointed brushes)
polymer gloss medium
pieces of 10 × 10" cardboard for storing reliefs

TEACHER PREPARATION

With help of students, collect and display photographs of jungle foliage. Prepare ball of clay for each student.

PROCEDURES

Session 1

Review and discuss various shapes found in jungle foliage. Discuss how shapes overlap to create shallow depth. Point out various patterns found in shapes.

Demonstrate how to make an 8" × 8" line drawing of jungle foliage to serve as a basis for clay relief of similar size. This is a working drawing, so basic shapes are more important than details at this point. Definite contours are important for easy transfer to clay. Ask students to make a variety of jungle shapes and at least three layers of overlapping foliage. The entire drawing surface should be filled with jungle shapes.

Blacken the back of the drawing or use carbon paper to transfer it to another sheet. Shapes on this sheet will be cut out and used as a pattern for clay shapes. The original drawing will serve as a guide for the clay relief.

Point out the importance of clearly differentiated shapes and how variety will reduce the confusion of similar shapes in different layers.

Session 2

Review key terms: contour, overlap, layers, and variety of shapes.

Carefully cut shapes from transferred drawing.

Cover work surface with plastic. Using approximately one half of the ball of clay, demonstrate how to flatten clay into an 8″ square slab about one-half inch thick.

From the remaining clay make a smaller and thinner slab. Cut out clay shapes from the smaller slab using patterns from transfer drawing and attach these shapes to 8″ square slab. Place the slabs on wooden squares for easier handling. Pay attention to layers and corresponding overlapping shapes.

Demonstrate how cutout shapes are attached to the slab by scoring each clay piece, brushing it with a small amount of water, and pressing the cutout onto the slab, creating at least three levels of overlapping foliage.

Relief shapes with patterns will require texture or additional surface detail. These should be added after the foliage has been attached to the slab. Textures can be created by adding clay to foliage shapes or by drawing patterns on the clay.

Finished clay reliefs should be initialed, placed on cardboard, loosely wrapped in plastic bags, and permitted to dry slowly.

Once pieces are thoroughly dry, they should be fired in a kiln to 1500°F.

Session 3

Discuss how clay reliefs will be further decorated with paints.

Before painting the fired clay reliefs, students should soak them in water to lessen absorbancy. Have students apply base coat of white tempera paint, taking care to fill in all cracks and edges. When dry, have students apply final colors. Practice mixing colors before painting clay relief is recommended. Dry plaques may be coated with a layer of polymer gloss medium and mounted on wood squares (¼″ plywood).

NOTE   If additional clay is available, make slabs 10″ × 10″.

SEE COLOR PLATE 39

PAPIER-MÂCHÉ PUPPET OF EXPRESSIVE CHARACTER

MATERIALS

newspaper strips (1″ widths, approximately 6″ long)
wheat paste
buckets
fine sandpaper
tempera paint
brushes
tagboard or stiff paper
scissors
fabric scraps, yarn, and other costume materials
needle and thread

TEACHER PREPARATION

Collect several illustrated books on puppetry for students to examine. If available in your school, *The Art of the Puppet* by Baird is an excellent reference book.

Prepare wheat paste and tear newspaper.

PROCEDURES

Session 1

Ask individual students to make faces expressing different moods—surprised, angry, joyful, brave, sad, powerful, wicked, mean, funny, excited, etc. Ask the class to guess what expression is being shown. Talk about characteristics the faces have that make them look sad, happy, angry, etc. Tell students they are going to make puppets with similar expressions or moods. Puppets can depict certain characters in books children have read which suggest a particular emotion or mood.

Demonstrate how to make papier-mâché puppet. First make the base or neck out of rolled tagboard, or a cardboard tube. Use tape to secure the cylinder. Make the neck wide and short enough for two fingers to control puppet head.

Make the basic shape of the head by wadding newspaper into desired shape and tape to neck.

Secure the head to cylinder by draping strips of newspaper dipped in wheat paste over the newspaper shape, gathering them at the neck of

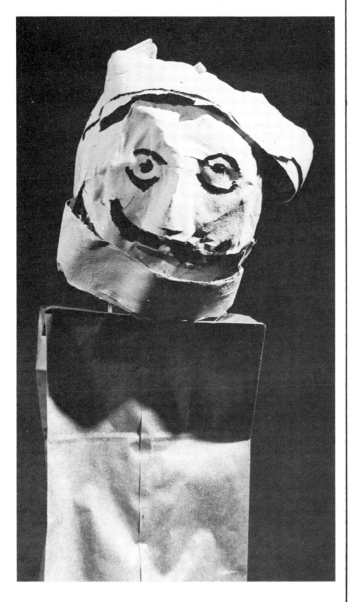

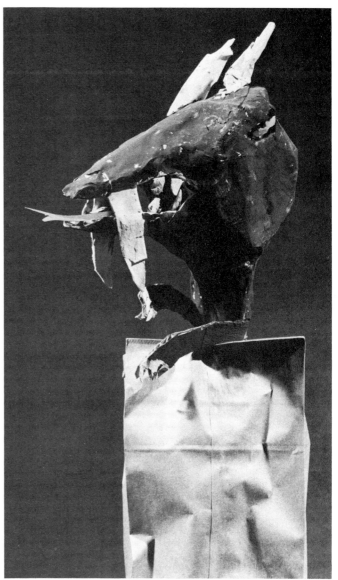

the cylinder. Dip pieces one at a time, remove excess paste, smooth, then add other pieces. If too much paste is used, small, dry pieces can be added to soak up the excess.

Session 2

Review the discussion about expressions and gestures. Have students select a particular expression or mood for their puppet or select a character which suggests a particular mood. Talk about the difference in shapes of noses, ears, chin, etc. Refer to illustrations. Concentrate on adding facial features that protrude and form a three-dimensional effect.

Demonstrate how to add features like nose and mouth by building up with small pieces of wadded newspaper and attaching with strips of newspaper and wheat paste.

After two layers of newspaper have been applied to the puppet head, apply a third layer of paper towel strips. When dry, use sandpaper to smooth rough edges.

Session 3

Paint puppet with a base coat of white tempera paint. Before adding other colors discuss what colors suggest particular moods or emotions (red for anger or embarrassment, blue for gloom or fear, yellow for brightness and happiness, gray for wickedness or evil, etc.). Paint puppets using color to convey desired mood or emotion.

Session 4

Sew and attach fabric scraps to puppet head to cover hand and to serve as a body for puppet. Yarn, excelsior, construction paper, steel wool, and other materials may be used for hair.

NOTES   Construction of puppets may take more than three sessions.

Students should wear a smock or old shirt when working with wheat paste.

A puppet stage may be constructed from large cardboard sheets, or simply use teacher's desk or table top for a stage. Students should write short skits based on the moods or emotions suggested by their puppets.

CLAY RELIEF FISH

MATERIALS   balls of clay (large grapefruit size), 1 for each student
clay tools, particularly knives and forks, for cutting and scoring
wood squares for mounting finished products (optional)
plastic bags
water buckets, sponges
tempera paints
brushes (1″ flat bristle and small pointed brushes)
10 × 10″ cardboards for storing reliefs
polymer gloss medium
pencils, erasers

TEACHER PREPARATION   Collect and display photographs of common fish. If available in your school, SVE visuals are excellent for this purpose (see Appendix C).

If available in school, display a fish bowl with live fish, plants, and seashells.

Prepare ball of clay for each student.

Ask students to collect buttons, thimbles, spools, nuts, bolts, screws, paper clips, and other found objects.

PROCEDURES   **Session 1**

Using visual aids, discuss the appearance of the fish. Point out the variety of shapes and surface patterns found in fish.

Cover the work surface with plastic. Using approximately half the ball of clay, flatten it into a 9″ square slab ½″ thick. Repeat process with the remaining clay. When two slabs have been made, explain additive building process students will use to make fish. Draw outline of fish shape on one slab, cut and place fish shape on top of second slab.

Demonstrate how to score surfaces to be joined. Use water sparingly for moistening.

After students have selected fish shapes from visuals, pass out materials and have students make slabs, draw cutout, and join to base slab. The fish shape should be large enough to cover most of the base slab.

When students have finished making their slabs, explain that the next step is to add various textures to the surface of the fish. Describe *texture* as the way a surface feels, for instance, rough or smooth (see Appendix B). Point out various textures in the classroom. Pass around an object rich in textural variations for students to feel. Demonstrate how to create different textures on the fish by pressing found objects into moist clay surface. Ask students to use at least three different shapes.

Have students place initials on back and loosely wrap plaques in plastic for slow drying. Store on pieces of cardboard to keep flat. After projects have thoroughly dried (approximately one to two weeks) they should be fired in a kiln to 1500°F.

Session 2

Before painting, have students briefly immerse projects in water to make them less absorbent. Instruct students to cover the entire relief surface, including edges, with a base coat of white tempera paint. After the base coat has thoroughly dried, use a minimum of four paint colors to add surface details.

When paint is completely dry, cover plaques with a layer of polymer gloss medium for a protective glossy coating. Finished reliefs may be mounted on wood squares (¼″ plywood) with epoxy glue.

SEE COLOR PLATE 40

81

CLAY RELIEF ANIMAL

MATERIALS

balls of clay (grapefruit size), 1 for each student
wood squares for displaying finished products (optional)
10 × 10″ cardboards
plastic bags
water buckets, sponges
clay tools, including plastic knives and forks, for cutting and scoring
tempera paints
brushes (1″ flat bristle and small pointed brushes)
polymer gloss medium

TEACHER PREPARATION

Display photographs of mammals and reptiles whose skins and fur have different textures (lamb, porcupine, alligator, armadillo, lizard, turtle).

Prepare ball of clay for each student.

Collect examples of materials and objects with various textures.

PROCEDURES

Session 1

Introduce textures by playing a feeling game. Have students identify items in a bag by touch only (i.e, by putting a hand into the bag and feeling each item). Define the word *texture* as the way a surface feels. See Appendix B for words describing texture.

Show reproductions of various mammals and reptiles with textural variations. Tell students that they are going to make a clay relief of a mammal or reptile.

Demonstrate how to flatten ball of clay into two slabs ½″ thick and approximately 6″ × 9″. Explain that one slab will serve as the base for the relief animal. For easier handling, work with clay on plastic surface. After making two slabs, have students select a mammal or reptile for their relief. An outline of the animal should be drawn on a slab, cut out, and mounted on base slab.

When students have successfully mounted their relief animal on the base slab, demonstrate how to make several textural surfaces by adding clay strips or coils to the animal shape. Demonstrate how the clay surfaces can be scored and pressed together. Use water sparingly. Have students *add* appropriate texture to their mammal or reptile. Caution students that clay pieces which are added to the animal shape must be securely attached and must be no thicker than ¼″. The textural surface should be dense.

When finished, loosely wrap the clay pieces with plastic and store on piece of cardboard. Allow the clay pieces to dry for a week or more. Once reliefs are thoroughly dry, fire slowly in kiln to 1500°F.

Session 2

Students should briefly immerse the fired clay reliefs in water to make them less absorbent. Instruct students to cover entire surface with a base coat of white tempera paint. Once the base coat is dry, the surface is ready for painting with assorted tempera colors.

Coat reliefs with polymer gloss medium. Finished reliefs may be mounted on wood squares (¼″ plywood) with epoxy glue.

SEE COLOR PLATE 41

83

LESSONS
FOR GRADES
5-6

CONSTRUCTION PAPER CARICATURE

MATERIALS

12″ × 18″ newsprint
pencils (#2)
small mirrors
erasers
scissors
white glue
12″ × 18″ construction paper, black and assorted colors

TEACHER PREPARATION

Several days before you teach this lesson, ask students to begin collecting cartoon caricatures and magazine photographs of political, sports, and entertainment figures found in news magazines and newspapers. Show some examples of good caricatures before making assignment.

Magazine photographs of faces will be necessary to make comparisons between actual photographs and caricatures. Several examples of magazine photographs and caricatures of the same individual will be most useful.

Set up a display of both caricatures and magazine photographs for reference during lesson.

PROCEDURES

Session 1

Referring to the display of photographs and caricatures, discuss how caricatures differ from photographs. Describe how caricature tells us about ourselves by paying special attention to certain parts of our face. Discuss the purpose of caricature in the news magazines and newspapers.

Discuss how caricature is achieved by exaggerating one or more of our facial features (shape of face, distance between eyes, shape of mouth and neck, length of nose, size of nostrils, hair style, size and shape of ears, etc.). Show a magazine photograph and a caricature of the same person. Point out how the caricature has exaggerated certain facial features (such as size of nose, teeth, and mouth) by making them much larger than they normally appear. Indicate to students that their own facial features can be used as the basis of a caricature. Ask students to look into hand mirrors and describe what features make their faces special and unique. Discuss how they would go about caricaturing themselves.

Have students use newsprint and pencils to draw self-portraits which make one or two of their facial features twice as large as they normally appear. Other features should be normal size. Portraits should be frontal, and life size. Have students use the mirror to study their face shapes carefully while drawing. Include neck and shoulders in the portrait.

Session 2

After drawing has been completed to student's satisfaction, a number 2 pencil should be used to blacken the back of the drawing. The student then traces the drawing onto black construction paper. Carefully cut facial, neck, and shoulder shapes from black paper and reposition on a separate piece of brightly colored construction paper. The lines of the original drawing have now become the outlines of solid shapes, which make a bold and dramatic caricature. This procedure also allows students to consider further exaggerations by repositioning features and examining relationships before gluing.

MOOD PORTRAIT COLLAGE

MATERIALS   pencils and erasers
scissors
white glue
mirrors
magazines with colored reproductions

TEACHER PREPARATION   A few days before teaching the lesson, ask students to bring magazines from home. *Vogue, Mademoiselle, Glamour,* and other magazines with large photographs of faces are most useful.

From magazines cut several large frontal faces which represent different emotions or moods for class demonstration.

Prepare slips of paper with one adjective describing a mood or feeling for each member of the class. Have a dictionary available.

PROCEDURES   Explain that lesson involves assembling an unconventional portrait which expresses a particular mood or feeling.

Ask the class to explain how adjectives are used to describe feelings or moods.

Explain how each student will pick from a hat one adjective describing an emotion or feeling. Sample words are *happy, angry, sneaky, mysterious, sleepy, awake, thirsty, hot, excited, furious, frightened, surprised, mean, beautiful, ugly, strong, weak, sweet, ashamed, lively, joyful, etc.* Tell students not to let anyone else in the class see their adjectives.

Ask how faces can be used to express emotions. Have a few students mime certain feelings or moods. Discuss the characteristics of facial expressions.

Tell students they will make a life size collage portrait using parts of faces cut from magazine photographs to express the particular mood or emotion written on their slip.

Demonstrate neat cutting and how to spread glue thinly and evenly so that it will not wrinkle the paper.

88

Review procedures for the lesson. Remind students not to let other students see their adjective so that class members can guess what emotion or feeling each portrait represents.

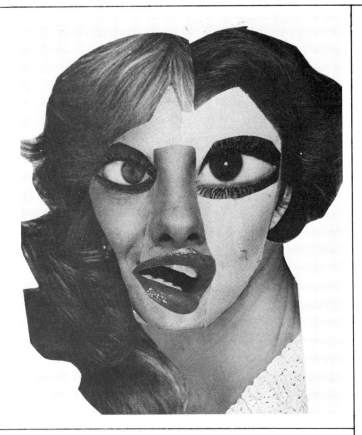

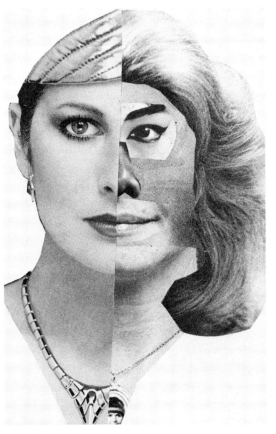

SEE COLOR PLATE 42

MACHINE PARTS TISSUE PAPER COLLAGE

MATERIALS

scissors
pencils and erasers
18″ × 24″ white drawing paper
12″ × 18″ newsprint
black felt-tip markers
white glue thinned with water
1″ brushes
tissue paper, assorted colors
polymer gloss medium

TEACHER PREPARATION

With help of students, collect examples of machine parts (gears, fans, junkyard materials) and arrange them into a still life composition.

PROCEDURES

Session 1

This project involves careful examination of tools and machines and their intricate parts. The drawing requires overlapping of shapes, filling the entire page with objects running off the page.

Have students examine the still life set-ups closely, and observe the variety of shapes and how they overlap.

Explain that most objects are formed from a combination of simple basic shapes (square, circle, rectangle). Have the students name the basic shapes found in the objects on display.

Ask students to make two or three small preliminary sketches of a still life on newsprint with pencils. Remind students to fill entire page with still life shapes. Ask students to select their best drawing and transfer it to 18″ × 24″ white drawing paper.

Session 2

After the pencil drawing is completed, retrace shapes with black felt markers.

Use drawings as guides for applying the tissue paper. To simplify color, students should work with three colors: three cools (blue/green/purple) or three warms (red/orange/yellow). Attach torn tissue pieces to paper by brushing over and under pieces with water-thinned glue. After entire collage is dry, a thin coat of polymer gloss medium may be applied over the entire picture for a protective glossy finish.

Use felt markers over tissue paper again to reemphasize lines.

NOTES　Brushes should not be permitted to dry while coated with polymer medium. Wash thoroughly with warm (not hot) water and soap.

Project may take more than two class sessions to finish.

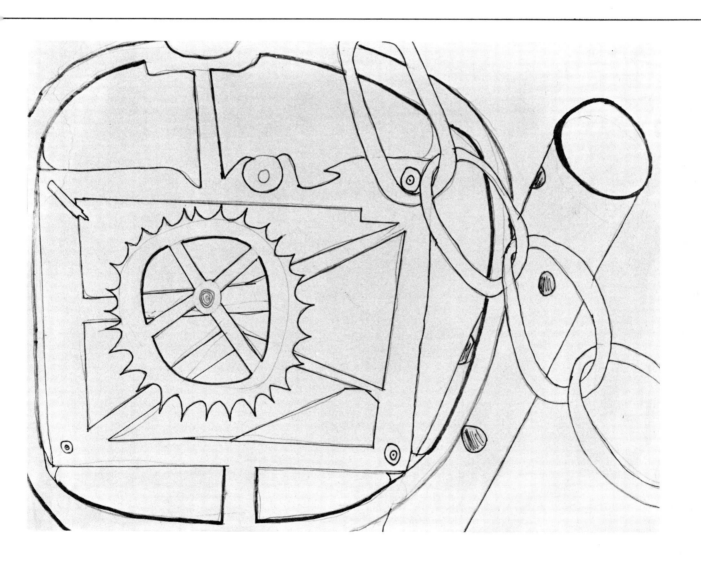

SEE COLOR PLATES 43–45

STILL LIFE TISSUE PAPER COLLAGE

MATERIALS

pencils and erasers
white glue
wide black felt-tip markers
tissue paper, assorted colors
viewfinders (4″ × 6″ cards with 1″ × 1½″ window)
brushes (1″ flat bristle)
buckets, sponges
scissors
12″ × 18″ white drawing paper

TEACHER PREPARATION

Set up still life (see Lesson 42 for suitable items).

Dilute white glue (1 part glue to 2 parts water) and pour into several containers.

PROCEDURES

Session 1

Discuss the arrangement of forms in the still life, noting overlapping, partially seen shapes, and proportional relationships. Demonstrate how to use viewfinders. Explain to students that they are to draw only those still life shapes which can be seen through viewfinders. Drawing should fill the entire page. If the viewfinder is held with its window horizontal, then the drawing paper should also be horizontal.

Have students make a contour line drawing of still life. Draw only those lines that define the outside edge of the shapes in still life. Draw only the portion of the still life which can be seen through viewfinder. Drawing should fill the entire page.

Session 2

Tissue paper should be cut to match shapes in drawing. Allow students to select colors freely. Apply tissue paper to completed contour line drawing with diluted glue mixture. Brush adhesive on both sides of tissue paper.

Session 3

When colors have been applied, instruct students to use black felt-tip markers to outline shapes in original drawing.

NOTE   Use of viewfinders allows the students to make a concentrated, detailed drawing of selected parts of the still life while eliminating unnecessary background.

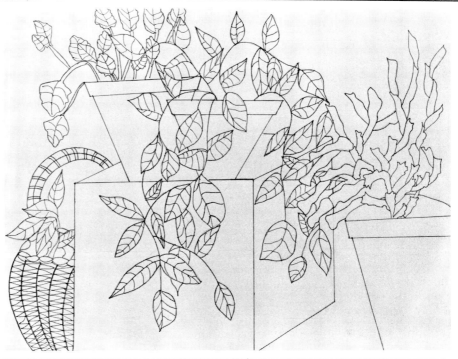

SEE COLOR PLATE 46

93

COLLAGE MURAL OF OUR TOWN

MATERIALS
10 feet of 36″ brown rolled kraft paper, for background
white drawing paper, assorted sizes
tempera paints, assorted colors
brushes (1″ flat bristle and small pointed brushes)
pencils and erasers
glue
containers for paint
mixing pans (aluminum pie plates)
water containers, sponges
scissors

TEACHER PREPARATION
Collect visuals of storefronts, houses, highrise buildings, police station, fire station, schools, automobiles, buses, churches, synagogues, trucks, trash cans, traffic lights, parking meters, flags, trees, shrubbery, and other items commonly seen in business and residential areas of town.

Cut white drawing paper into three different sizes: 18″×24″, 9″×12″, and 6″×9″.

PROCEDURES
Session 1

Explain to class that they are going to make a collage mural of our town.

Involve class in discussion about the various kinds of man-made and natural objects found in our town.

With the help of children, list on board the specific objects to be included: building shapes (houses, stores, police and fire stations, churches); modes of transportation (cars, buses, airplanes, trucks); and other miscellaneous items (trash cans, traffic lights, parking meters, flags, trees, shrubbery, streets, sidewalks, grass, sky, clouds).

Have students examine differences in the shapes and proportions of objects listed on board. Classify the objects as small, medium, large, or huge (the number of categories depends on how many paper sizes are available for the lesson).

Discuss the general design, location, and size of items for the mural.

94

Divide students into groups responsible for making examples of various kinds and sizes of items: commercial buildings, public buildings, transportation, residences, natural objects, miscellaneous objects. Appoint one student to be chairperson of each group.

Students should begin by drawing the outline of the object, paying special attention to details and size relationships previously discussed. Opaque tempera paint should be used for colors. Encourage students to paint details last. When objects are dry they should be cut out and stored.

Session 2

This session is devoted to assembling the mural by attaching the cutouts to the kraft paper background. Have chairpersons of various groups serve as mural organizers. Unroll the background paper and place flat on floor. The arrangement of objects on the background should begin by attaching roads, grass, and sky. Other objects should be carefully placed on surface before gluing. Special consideration should be given to overlapping shapes and placement of items. Once the general design of the mural is agreed upon, items should be carefully glued in place.

Caution students to apply glue evenly in order to avoid ugly lumps and damage to paint surface.

SEE COLOR PLATE 47

BICYCLE PARTS DRAWING

MATERIALS
12″ × 18″ white drawing paper
pencils
erasers
viewfinders (4″ × 6″ stiff paper with 1″ × 1½″ window)
black felt-tip markers

TEACHER PREPARATION
Ask one or two students to bring bicycles to school for use as classroom drawing model. Set the bikes up in front of room.

PROCEDURES
Demonstrate how a viewfinder can be used to isolate and "frame" a part of a subject.

Explain that students are to draw only the part of the bike which they see through the viewfinder. Students should station themselves close enough to the bicycles so that only bicycle shapes can be seen through the viewfinder. Drawings should not include floor or background materials. Students should begin to perceive relationships by carefully examining every detail. Everything seen through the viewfinder should be drawn. For best results, viewfinders should be held at arm's length.

Have students match viewfinder window shape with paper shape (both should be held either vertically or horizontally). Allow students about forty minutes to make a light pencil line drawing. Stress continued use of the viewfinder and detailed observations of bicycle parts.

Demonstrate how to use the markers to make bold lines over pencil lines for the finished drawing.

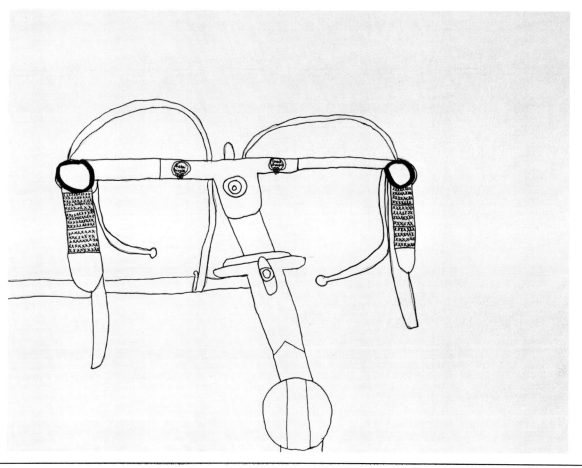

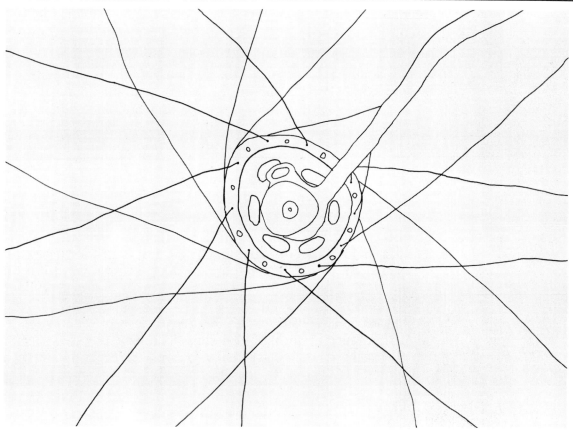

97

METAMORPHOSIS MARKER DRAWING

MATERIALS

9″ × 12″ white paper, 4 sheets for each student
fine felt-tip markers, assorted colors
oil pastels (optional)
pencils and erasers

TEACHER PREPARATION

With the help of students, collect and display examples of animate and inanimate objects which have similar shapes (see examples listed below).

PROCEDURES

Explain that *metamorphosis* means a transformation or change that occurs in a number of gradual but sequential steps. Discuss the metamorphosis of a butterfly as an example. Compare the shape of first stage of the butterfly (pupa) with the final stage (butterfly).

The assignment is to observe shape similarities between totally different objects. This will be accomplished by taking an inanimate object and, in several drawings, transform it into an animate object of similar shape, such as a teapot into elephant, study lamp into flower, stapler into alligator, or fire extinguisher into exotic bird. Review the meaning of *animate* and *inanimate*. Make a list on blackboard of some objects which have animate and inanimate counterparts that are similar in shape. Examples are elephant—pencil sharpener; daisy—electric fan; beetle—Volkswagen, porcupine—hairbrush. Students are to select one pair of objects that have a similar shape.

Have students begin by making pencil drawings of the objects they have chosen. Both inanimate and animate objects should be drawn the same size. The gradual transformations should occur in the second and third drawings. Since the first drawing is of an inanimate object, then the second drawing should have many of the features of the inanimate shape and a few features of the similar shaped animate object. Conversely, the third drawing should have many features of the animate shape and only a few features of the inanimate shape.

After four pencil drawings have been completed, have students use black marker to outline shapes and oil pastels to color.

98

SEE COLOR PLATES 48 AND 49

99

OIL PASTEL RESIST
OF FLOWER GARDEN
40

MATERIALS
12″ × 18″ light-colored construction paper
pencils
erasers
oil pastels
black and/or dark blue tempera paint
brushes (1″ flat bristle)
sponges

TEACHER PREPARATION
Display pictures of various types of garden flowers and foliage. If available in school, display some live plants in room.

PROCEDURES
Discuss plants found in a garden. Ask students to identify and describe differences among plants seen in the display.

Note variety of shapes and the overlapping of shapes. Point out that one way to get a crowded effect in a drawing is by overlapping and filling the entire space with flower shapes. Flower stems and leaves should be dense. Emphasize also the variety of sizes and colors in leaves and flowers. Ask students why the horizon line seen in pictures that show distance need not be present in pictures that show close-up views. Discuss.

Demonstrate how to mix colors with oil pastels. Stress pressing down firmly with oil pastels for rich solid color areas which will resist final coat of paint. Leave areas between flowers uncolored for resist color.

Demonstrate how to apply paint. With the flat bristle brush, apply paint using horizontal brushstrokes in one direction. Do not scrub or brush back and forth across the paper. Recoat for desired color richness. Remove excess paint with sponge. Oil pastel colors may be re-applied to intensify color relationships.

NOTE
Allow three sessions to complete lesson.

SEE COLOR PLATES 50 AND 51

INSECT CRAYON ENGRAVING

MATERIALS

crayons
9″ × 12″ oak tag paper
pencils
black tempera paint
brushes (1″ flat bristle)
containers for water and paint
liquid soap
pointed instruments (nails, paper clips, or compasses)

TEACHER PREPARATION

With the assistance of students, collect and display photographs of insects. Use SVE visuals (insect portfolio) if available in school (see Appendix C).

Make samples of crayon engravings at various stages: colored scribble drawing, drawing covered with tempera paint partially engraved.

PROCEDURES

Session 1

Tell students that this lesson will concentrate on using line to show a variety of visual patterns that are found within insect shapes and their immediate surroundings.

Examine patterns that can be seen in insect photographs. Show a finished crayon engraving. Define *crayon engraving* as scratching onto painted oak tag plate to reveal colored crayon areas underneath.

Demonstrate the crayon engraving process: Make a scribble drawing by using a light-colored crayon and drawing one continuous, flowing line intersecting at many points. Point out the variety of shapes created.

Fill in the areas with different colored crayons, applying evenly and thickly to cover white of paper. Use bright colors for best effects, but omit black and other dark colors. After coloring is completed, apply an even coat of creamy thick black tempera paint.

To help the paint stick to the waxy crayon, add about a tablespoonful of liquid soap to every pint of paint. Set aside to dry.

102

Sessions 2 and 3

When the oak tag plate is dry, students should make a pencil drawing of an insect on top of tempera surface. Careful attention should be given to outlining body markings and details. Encourage students to select insects with many lines or patterns. The insect shape should fill the drawing surface. Students may include shapes found in the insect's environment (branches, leaves) if space is available.

Demonstrate how to use a nail, paper clip end, or compass point to scratch away the paint to reveal the crayon underneath. See that newspapers are spread underneath this messy procedure.

Summarize by advising students to first scratch away the lines defining the insect shape. Scratch away the interior body markings or patterns next. The insect form should fill the entire page and students should be encouraged to remove approximately half of the black tempera paint covering in order to reveal the various colors underneath while retaining enough black to insure contrast.

NOTE This lesson should take at least three sessions to complete.

SEE COLOR PLATES 52 AND 53

DISTORTED STILL LIFE DRAWING

MATERIALS

18″ × 24″ white drawing paper
pencils (#2) and erasers
scissors
white glue
colored pencils
18″ × 24″ newsprint paper
thick and thin black felt-tip markers
rulers
masking tape

TEACHER PREPARATION

With the help of children, collect items which could be included in still life (bottles, boxes, jars, machine parts, lamp shades, umbrella, suitcases, fabric). Set up a still life arrangement that includes several overlapping objects. Locate centrally.

PROCEDURES

Session 1

Discuss how contour lines follow the outer edge of shapes. Allow about ten minutes for students to make a preliminary contour line sketch of the still life filling the entire page. In a discussion, have the students compare what they have drawn with what they actually see. Point out the size relationships among the various objects, and how objects overlap each other in a drawing to give the feeling of depth. Have students draw objects large enough to fill the page. Stress careful examination of shapes and proportions. Drawings should include overlapping shapes. When drawing is finished, go over lines with black marker. Blacken the back of drawing with number 2 pencil and trace entire drawing on a second piece of paper with pencil.

Session 2

Discuss what makes something distorted or exaggerated. Demonstrate how to distort traced drawings first by cutting out the object in the

traced drawing, then by further cutting various objects into several other shapes. While looking at the original drawing, reassemble the objects cut from the traced drawing so still life is distorted but still recognizable. Discuss how to achieve best distortion effects through decisions made in cutting up objects in drawings. When satisfied with arrangement, glue shapes to piece of white drawing paper.

Session 3

Indicate that in previous lessons distortion was achieved by cutting and rearranging shapes in drawing. Demonstrate that another type of distortion can be achieved by darkening in parts of both background shapes and the still life shapes in such a way as to achieve a checkerboard balance between light and dark areas.

Students should begin the session by tracing the distorted drawing done during the second session. After completing the light and dark pattern, student will have three drawings which show a sequence from reality to distortion.

NOTES Large, simple objects are best to use for the still lifes, because small, detailed objects will be too confusing to handle for the desired distortion effects.

Emphasize drawing the objects large enough to fill the page.

Students should keep cut-up shapes for Session 2 large enough to avoid confusing or losing portions of the composition.

EXPERIMENTAL LANDSCAPE PAINTING

MATERIALS

12″ × 18″ manila paper
pencils and erasers
tempera paints
brushes (1″ flat bristle, medium and small pointed brushes)
containers for paint
water buckets, sponges
mixing pans (aluminum pie plates)

TEACHER PREPARATION

With help of students, collect magazines with colored pictures of landscapes. Cut a 1″ × 3″ strip from colored landscape pictures for each class member. For best results, cut strips from pictures which include some part of horizon line, bright colors, and a variety of natural and landscape shapes. Avoid pictures with houses, other man-made shapes, and animals or human beings. Paste swatches near middle of horizontal 12″ × 18″ manila paper.

PROCEDURES

Tell students they are going to make an experimental painting by completing the landscape suggested by a color sample cut from a magazine picture and glued to manila paper. In addition to drawing lines and shapes to complete the landscape, the tempera colors used in the painting should be carefully mixed to match those on the color sample. In the finished painting, the color sample should blend into the rest of the painting.

Demonstrate how to mix colors to match those on a color sample similar to those which students will use. When mixing paints, darker colors should be added to the lighter colors; otherwise, more light color will be needed to make desired color. Also avoid using paint too watery or too thick.

Explain that students should paint the background area first, details later. Paint from most general to most detailed. Large brushes should be used for background areas, small brushes for details.

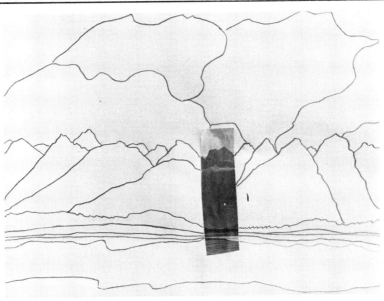

SEE COLOR PLATE 54

107

PATTERNED ANIMAL RELIEF PRINT

MATERIALS

9″ × 12″ flexible printing plates with adhesive backing
brayers
black water-base ink
inking plates (glass or plexiglass)
lino cutting tools and assorted cutting points
printing paper (or use newsprint, tissue, or construction paper)
6″ × 9″ newsprint
6″ × 9″ tagboard or noncorrugated cardboard
pencils (#2)
scissors
erasers

TEACHER PREPARATION

With the help of students, collect and display magazine pictures of animals. Avoid displaying pictures which present incomplete or hard to draw views of animals; side or frontal views are best. Before Session 3, set up a printing station for four to five students.

PROCEDURES

Session 1

After discussing the size and unique shapes found in the animal pictures displayed in class, have students make preliminary contour drawing of an animal of their choosing. Emphasize that only limited amounts of the animal's environment should be included in the drawing. Drawings should fill the entire piece of 6″ × 9″ newsprint.

When drawings are finished, demonstrate how to transfer them to a flexible printing plate by blacking out the lines on back of the sketch with a pencil and tracing by using carbon paper. Affix flexible printing plate to cardboard backing before proceeding. Save the original drawing.

Session 2

Demonstrate paper cutting procedure on scrap materials. Show how various points can be used to produce fine and thick cuts. An outline of the animal shape should be cut out first. Indicate that raised areas will print the same color as the ink while the cut-out areas will be the color of the paper. After students have cut out the animal shape, demon-

strate how to cut different patterns in the background areas and in the animal body by varying the shape, width, and density of the curls. Emphasize that students should always point cutting tools away from their bodies while gouging surface.

Tell students that before they cut pattern into the flexible printing plate they should draw some sample patterns on their original contour drawing. Indicate the importance of making animal patterns that contrast with background patterns. Approximately two-thirds of the surface of the flexible printing plate should be covered with cut patterns.

Session 3

Indicate to students that printing will be done by no more than four to five students at one time. Squeeze about one inch of water base ink onto inking plate, then demonstrate how brayer rolls ink evenly onto the inking plate with horizontal and vertical motions. Transfer the ink to the flexible printing plate surface with the brayer. Make sure the printing plate is evenly coated with ink. Lay printing paper over inked printing plate and transfer image to paper by rubbing with heel of hand or clean brayer.

Repeat the printing process using different types of paper.

NOTE Remember that water-based ink dries fast, so students should be encouraged to work quickly.

SEE COLOR PLATES 55–57

COLLAGRAPH PRINT OF STILL LIFE

MATERIALS
lino cutting tools and assorted cutting points
9″ × 12″ flexible printing plates with adhesive backing
inking plates (glass or plexiglass)
brayers
black water-base printing ink (other colors optional)
scraps of burlap, nylon, sandpaper, other textured materials
white glue
9″ × 12″ drawing paper
9″ × 12″ newsprint
tissue paper, assorted colors
9″ × 12″ tagboard or noncorrugated cardboard
scissors

TEACHER PREPARATION
Collect a variety of materials to use for still life set-up (see Lesson 42 for suitable items).

Set up still life in central location. Include several overlapping shapes.

Before Session 3, set up a printing station to accommodate no more than four to five students at one time.

PROCEDURES

Session 1

Discuss the organization of the still life, the various shapes, relationships and proportions, overlapping objects, and surfaces.

Have students make a contour line drawing of still life on 9″ × 12″ newsprint. Emphasize that drawing should fill the entire page. Instruct students to carefully observe shape, proportions, overlapping objects, and details of various still life objects. Remind students that a good drawing is required in order to get a good print.

Completed newsprint drawings should be transferred to the flexible printing plate. Drawings can be transferred by blackening the back of the drawing with pencil and then retracing the drawing with flexible plate underneath, or by using carbon paper.

111

Session 2

Cut still life shapes from the flexible printing plate with scissors, and glue to tagboard or cardboard.

Discuss the various surface patterns (stripes, checks, etc.) contained within the still life shapes. After demonstrating how to use the cutting tools, instruct students to create surface patterns found on still life objects. Avoid lettering. Show how prints will be the reverse of the image on the flexible plate. Remind students to point cutting tools away from their bodies while gouging out surface patterns. Have students make experimental patterns on scrap materials before cutting still life patterns. Background should be covered with pieces of burlap, nylon, sandpaper, or other textural materials to create surface patterns in the print.

Session 3

Demonstrate how to make prints. Squeeze about an inch of water base black ink onto inking plate. Move brayer vertically and horizontally to distribute ink evenly. Transfer ink onto the flexible printing plate with brayer. (It is unavoidable that the background will also receive modest amounts of ink.) Move plate to a clean place.

Lay a sheet of colored tissue paper with margins at least two inches larger than the printing plate over the plate. Smooth the tissue paper by hand and begin transferring the ink to the paper by rubbing over the paper with heel of hand. (A clean hard rubber brayer or wooden spoon may also be used.) Check the success of the transfer by picking up the corners of the paper. You will need to pull points fairly quickly when working with water base printing ink. Point out reverse image which results in printing. Set the print aside to dry.

NOTES   Students may use colored ink, different kinds of paper, and further modify the final print by using oil pastels or crayons.

For best results have small groups of students use printing station at one time. It would be helpful to have teacher's aid assist students during the actual printing phase.

CEREMONIAL CLAY MASK

MATERIALS

balls of clay (grapefruit size), 1 for each student
newspaper
buckets, sponges
drawing paper
pencils and erasers
10″ × 10″ cardboards
clay tools, including plastic knives and forks
plastic bags
tempera paints, assorted colors
brushes (1″ flat bristle and small pointed)
masking tape
polymer gloss medium

TEACHER PREPARATION

With the help of local librarian, collect and display resource materials, including photographs and drawings of early Indian artifacts (pottery, masks, totems, jewelry, etc.). Resource materials showing American Hopi and pre-Columbian artifacts would be most useful.

Ask children to help collect illustrations of various Indian arts and crafts.

Prepare ball of clay for each student.

PROCEDURES

Session 1

Use visuals to prompt discussion about various Indian cultures. Discuss the symbols, shapes, and patterns found in Indian artifacts (pottery, masks, totems, jewelry).

Explain that some Indians believed that animals, birds, and other objects embodied spirits or life forces. For example, the thunderbird made thunder by flapping its wings; the raven created the earth; the bear was the spirit of strength; the eagle, the spirit of hunting; the frog, the spirit of alertness. Indicate that Indian ceremonial masks were the forerunners of Halloween, Mardi Gras, and other festival masks. Tell students that they are going to make a ceremonial clay mask which combines human, animal, and bird features much like Indian masks and totem poles.

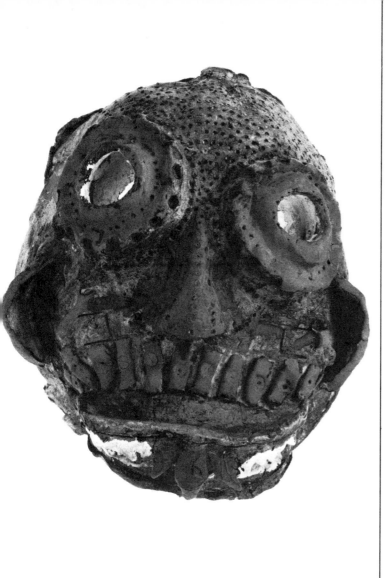

SEE COLOR PLATES 58 AND 59

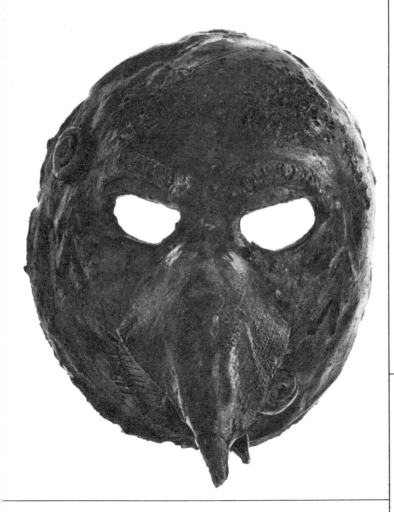

Working on a plastic surface, demonstrate how to make a square slab approximately 9″ × ½″ thick out of one-half ball of clay. Wet several pieces of newspaper and shape like an upside-down oval bowl approximately 4″ high, 6″ wide, and 8″ long. Demonstrate how to drape clay slabs over newspaper support to form the curved mask shape. When this phase of the project is complete, make slabs airtight by covering with plastic. Place each slab on piece of cardboard with student's name and store.

Session 2

Have students examine beaks, ears, eyes, horns, snouts, teeth, tongues, and other features found in resource materials. Encourage students to select various combinations of features for their masks.

Uncover draped slab made during previous session. Demonstrate how to cut out edges of slab to make oval face shape. Demonstrate how to construct and attach animal and bird features for ceremonial masks.

Have students make features protrude from mask surface. Masks should be finished by adding surface patterns and textures. Show examples of Indian patterns, noting geometric forms. Explain that the surface patterns and textures can be created by *adding* clay strips, coils, circles, and triangles to the clay surface. When masks are finished, have students carve name on back. Cover loosely with plastic for slow drying, place on piece of cardboard and let dry for two weeks. Then fire slowly in kiln to 1500°F.

Session 3

Color will be used only to highlight areas of the mask. First, stain entire mask with brown tempera paint thinned with water. Wipe off excess with sponge. Add a second or third coat to darken recessed areas.

Highlight important features with bright tempera colors—the edges of eyes, mouth, patterns, ears, and horns. Use paint sparingly or surface patterns and textures may be obscured.

After paint is dry, apply a layer of polymer gloss medium to seal paint.

NOTE   This project may require more than three sessions to complete.

LIFE SIZE THREE-DIMENSIONAL SELF-PORTRAIT

MATERIALS

paper plates (9″ size)
1 set of each child's clothing—if possible have girls bring slacks instead of a dress. Old clothing is advisable.
construction paper, assorted colors
white glue
yarn
small mirrors
newspapers for stuffing
stapler and staples, safety pins
wire coat hangers

TEACHER PREPARATION

With the help of the class, collect examples of frontal portraits, some showing just the face and some showing the entire body. Set up display in class for reference during project.

PROCEDURES

Session 1

Discuss and compare shapes and sizes of heads and facial features of portrait examples. Note also placement of facial features.

Show where to place the features on the head in a demonstration drawing on the chalkboard.

Demonstrate how to cut facial features from construction paper. Organize and glue them on the back surface of one paper plate covered with piece of skin-colored construction paper. Demonstrate how to glue yarn to the back of the other plate to suggest hair. Stress detailed observation and careful placement of facial features. Don't forget teeth, eyelashes, ears, eyebrows, cheeks, and hair styles. Have hand mirrors available for students to use when making features.

After both sides of the head are finished, demonstrate how to staple the two plates together.

Session 2

When students have finished paper plate portraits they can stuff their clothing with old newspapers. Use newspaper to stuff clothing in order

118

to make it look real and life size. Attach body parts to each other and keep stuffing in place with pins and staples.

A wire coat hanger inserted into each shirt as it is being stuffed will permit convenient storage and display. It is a good idea to do the stuffing during the last period of the day.

NOTE This project is most successful during open house for parents. When the parents enter the classroom they can find their "children" sitting in their seats.

SEE COLOR PLATE 60

IMAGINARY MACHINE SCULPTURE

MATERIALS   large assortment of small wood scraps
hammers, finish nails
white glue
cardboard
fine sandpaper
stovepipe wire
black tempera paint
brushes

TEACHER PREPARATION   With help of children, collect and display pictures of machines and machine parts from automotive magazines, farm machinery advertising materials, etc.

Collect small wood scraps, usually available free from the local lumber yard or high school wood scraps. The largest scrap should be no bigger than six inches. Smaller scraps with unusual shapes are desirable. High school shop teachers can be helpful in preparing scraps for this lesson.

PROCEDURES   Define *sculpture* as three-dimensional art forms which usually can be seen from all sides. Tell students they are going to make sculptures of imaginary machines from wood scraps. The machines won't really work, of course, but they will look like machines.

Explain that the first part to be made is a stand to support the machine. Point out that candy machines, pinball machines, drill presses, and sewing machines all have a stand. Have students design a platform or stand for their machine. Platform must be stable and well balanced. While glue will be adequate for attaching most of the scraps, hammer and nails might be needed for construction of the stand.

The body of the machine itself should involve at least ten pieces of scrap wood. Scraps should be organized to suggest machine parts, for example, small pieces of cardboard may be cut for gear shapes, or wire may be added to suggest fan belts.

For a more unified appearance, assembled machines should be painted with black tempera paint when glue is hard.

Students may bring small objects from home to make their machines more convincing, such as small gear parts, spring, bolts, etc.

Depending on complexity of machines, project should take two or more sessions to complete.

FREE-STANDING TEXTURED CLAY ANIMAL

MATERIALS

balls of clay (grapefruit size), 1 for each student
clay tools, including plastic knives and forks
buckets, sponges
plastic bags
tempera paint (brown)
brushes (large flat bristle and small pointed)
polymer gloss medium (optional)
10″ × 10″ cardboards

TEACHER PREPARATION

With the help of children, collect and display pictures of various domestic and wild animals with varied textural surfaces. Ask students to choose pictures which reveal the complete animal shape (side or frontal views are best).

Prepare ball of clay for each student.

Collect examples of materials and objects with various textures.

PROCEDURES

Session 1

Show pictures of a variety of animals with textural variations. Tell students that they are going to make a free-standing clay sculpture of a textural animal. Point out sizes, shapes, unique features, and surface textures of various animals.

Working on a plastic covered surface, demonstrate how to first make a body by shaping with hands, then add legs, head, tail, and other features. Demonstrate scoring and joining techniques. To speed up drying time and to prevent damage, clay shapes should be hollowed out if they are thicker than ¾″. Caution students to make small airholes in enclosed hollow forms.

When body shape is finished, wrap animal shape in airtight plastic bag. Place on cardboard with student's name, and store.

Session 2

Referring to the pictures of animals on display, demonstrate how to make several textures by *adding* clay coils, circles, and other shapes to the animal surface.

Before adding appropriate textures to their animals, have students recheck clay joints. Clay textures must be securely attached and should be no thicker than ¼″. Textural areas should be dense.

When finished, have students place initials on bottom of animals and loosely wrap in plastic. Allow to dry for two weeks. When pieces are thoroughly dry, fire slowly in kiln to 1500°F.

Session 3

Have students briefly immerse fired animal shapes in water to make less absorbant. Stain the entire animal surface with brown tempera paint thinned with water. Wipe off excess with sponge. Add a second or third coat to darken recessed areas. After paint is dry, apply coat of polymer gloss medium to seal.

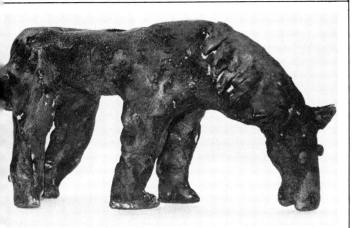

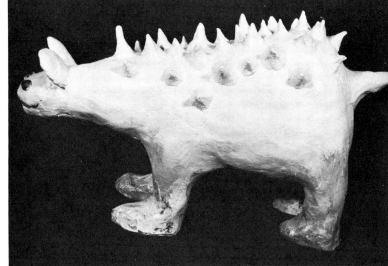

ANIMAL FIGURE WIRE SCULPTURE

MATERIALS

30″ lengths of soft wire (stovepipe or other flexible yet substantial wire)
wire cutters or pliers with cutting edge
wood blocks, approximately 4″ × 6″
black tempera paint (optional)
u-tacks and hammer

TEACHER PREPARATION

With the help of students, collect and display pictures of animals and humans in motion.

PROCEDURES

Referring to pictures on display, discuss how parts of the body bend to suggest motion. With the help of a class member "frozen" in various action poses, point out the position of arms and legs and point of balance when the body is running, jumping, bending, etc. Compare with body not in motion. Tell students they are going to make wire sculptures of animals or figures which suggest motion.

Demonstrate how wire can be twisted and bent to create three-dimensional skeletal forms which are balanced to suggest certain gestures and motions.

Demonstrate how to cut wire and how to join pieces of wire by wrapping and twisting with fingers. Show how to attach finished wire sculptures to wooden base with u-tacks. If desired, base may be painted with black tempera paint before attaching sculpture.

NOTES

Tell students to use wire as if it were a pencil, making twisting, circular lines in the air.

This project may require two sessions to complete.

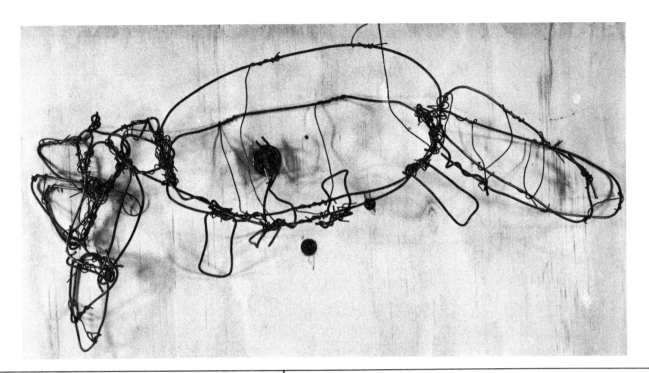

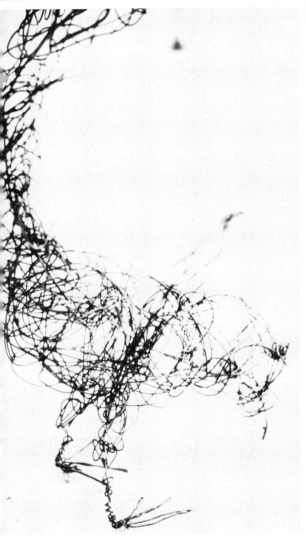

125

EFFIGY POTTERY

MATERIALS

balls of clay (grapefruit size) 1 for each student
plastic bags
water buckets, sponges
clay tools, including plastic knives and forks
tempera paints (brown)
brushes (large flat bristle and small pointed)
polymer gloss medium (optional)
10″ × 10″ cardboards

TEACHER PREPARATION

Refer to materials collected for the ceremonial clay mask project (Lesson 46). Display photographs and books of pottery masks and totems. Look for other examples of pottery that combine animal and human surface decorations with functional pottery forms.

Prepare ball of clay for each student.

PROCEDURES

Session 1

Using resource materials collected for this activity, discuss the purpose of effigy objects in early societies. Tell students that effigy pots are clay containers which have human or animal characteristics. In addition to serving as containers for liquids and other materials, effigy pots have certain symbolic purposes which are magical, religious, or ceremonial. They can represent particular *spirits* (fertility, hunt, love), *events* (planting, harvesting), and *rituals* (birth, death, worship).

Begin by making several ½″ slab shapes by hand flattening or rolling the clay with dowel or rolling pin. Point out that effigy pottery can be made by several clay building techniques, but the one that we will use is a combination of slab and coil technique. Demonstrate how to construct a functional container by rolling slabs into a cylindrical shape. (Rectangular and square shapes can also be used.) Attach ends of slab and base by scoring and overlapping edges. Press small coils into joints to add stability. Point out that the particular effigy shapes chosen will determine the shape of functional purposes—beaks and snouts can be pouring spouts in pitcher or teapots, tails and ears can be handles.

126

SEE COLOR PLATE 61

Students should be instructed to begin by selecting an effigy image. Ask students to reexamine the resource materials on display for ideas. Once an image has been selected, the basic container shape should be constructed. If sides of container begin to sag, the clay is too soft and piece should be set aside for short period of time.

When this phase of the project is complete, make shapes airtight by covering with plastic, place on piece of cardboard with student's name, and store.

Session 2

Before adding human and animal features and other details, have students recheck joints on container shape. Encourage students to exaggerate the size of features. Make them protrude from container surface. Attached pieces should be no more than ½" thick.

Pots should be finished by adding appropriate textures. When effigy pots are finished, have students carve names on bottom. Cover loosely with plastic for slow drying and let dry for two weeks. Fire slowly in kiln to 1500°F.

Session 3

Briefly immerse in water to make less absorbant. Have students stain entire mask with brown tempera paint thinned with water. Wipe off excess with damp sponge. Add second and third coats to darken recessed areas.

Use bright tempera colors sparingly to highlight the edges of features. When tempera paint is dry, apply coat of polymer gloss medium to seal paint.

NOTE   This project may require more than three sessions to complete.

FANTASY BIRD SCULPTURE

MATERIALS
18″ × 24″ white drawing paper
oil pastels
black tempera paint
scissors
mixing pans
newspaper
paper hole punch

TEACHER PREPARATION
Several days before lesson, ask students to bring colored pictures of birds to class (suggest looking through old issues of *National Wildlife, National Geographic, World,* etc.).

If available in your school, display examples from the Reinhold Visuals Portfolio 4, Surface, and Society for Visual Education prints of common birds and familiar birds (see Appendix C).

PROCEDURES
Prominently display collected pictures of birds.

Introduce lesson with a discussion of birds seen near school. Make a list of birds students identify. After examining the birds on display, discuss the characteristics that make birds different from each other. Ask several questions about shapes, colors, body markings or patterns, and proportions.

Explain that the purpose of the lesson is to draw and construct a stuffed paper sculpture of an imaginary bird, using oil pastel resist process to decorate the surface. Make sure class understands sculpture as a three-dimensional art.

Discuss different ways students can construct an imaginary bird: by exaggerating certain shapes, colors, and patterns found in existing birds; by varying the size and shape of the wings, body, beak, tail, eyes, feet, colors, and body markings; by interchanging parts from known birds.

Demonstrate how to draw a profile or side view of an imaginary bird by combining and exaggerating the features of several bird shapes.

Demonstrate how to construct the bird shape from paper: Fold paper in half; draw side view of imaginary bird on one side of the folded paper as large as possible; cut out outline of bird through the double thickness of paper, thus creating two bird shapes. Do not make the legs and neck of birds too thin.

Demonstrate how to draw surface patterns representing exaggerated body markings on both of the cut bird shapes. Color body markings with oil pastels. Have students use a variety of colors and apply even pressure to the oil pastels to make solid color areas. A reasonable balance should be achieved between the areas which are colored with oil pastels and areas which are left plain. (At least half the area should be colored.)

After coloring is completed, black tempera paint should be brushed over the entire surface of both cutouts. The areas colored with oil pastels will resist the paint, thus creating an attractive batik effect.

After the paint dries, the two cutouts of the bird should be stapled partially together, then stuffed with newspaper before being entirely stapled.

NOTE   Allow at least two sessions to complete project.

SEE COLOR PLATE 62

131

CARDBOARD BOX AND CONSTRUCTION PAPER SCULPTURE

MATERIALS

12″ × 18″ construction paper, assorted colors
scissors
white glue
tissue paper, assorted colors
pencils
masking tape
assorted boxes

TEACHER PREPARATION

Select several stories which thoroughly describe and illustrate examples of imaginary characters in children's literature.

Several weeks before teaching the lesson ask students to collect a wide variety of small boxes (cylindrical oats boxes, rectangular cereal boxes, egg boxes, etc.). A visit to a drugstore cosmetics counter will yield an assortment of well-constructed, small boxes.

PROCEDURES

Session 1

After reading several brief passages which describe imaginary characters in children's literature, select one or two well-known characters and ask students to analyze which combination of basic shapes (rectangles, cylinders, squares, cones) could be used to construct a simplified version of the character. Stress the importance of initially examining the characters in terms of simple undecorated shapes. Details, costumes, and decorations can be added after basic structure has been carefully constructed.

List various imaginary characters from children's literature, such as those from *Alice's Adventures in Wonderland, Charlotte's Web, Wizard of Oz, Just So Stories,* and *Grimm's Fairy Tales.* It may be useful to have students reread descriptive passages about their favorite characters before making sculpture.

Demonstrate how the boxes which have been collected by students can be combined and modified to construct imaginary characters. Demonstrate how to attach boxes by gluing, tabbing, and taping.

SEE COLOR PLATES 63 AND 64

Ask students to select boxes necessary to construct their character. Boxes with unwanted advertising on surfaces should be covered with construction paper.

Session 2

Once the basic structure has been completed, costumes, facial features, and other details should be added by attaching construction paper, tissue paper, cloth, aluminum foil, and other materials to the form.

Demonstrate cutting, scoring, curling, and other paper sculpture techniques.

NOTE   This lesson may require more than two sessions to complete.

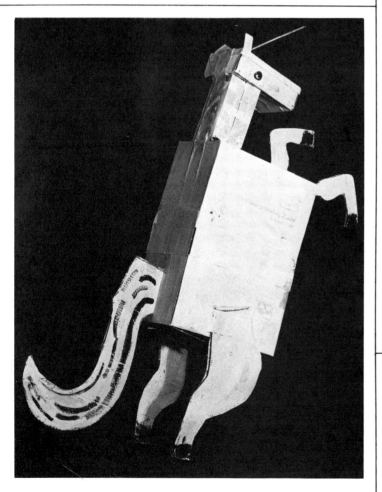

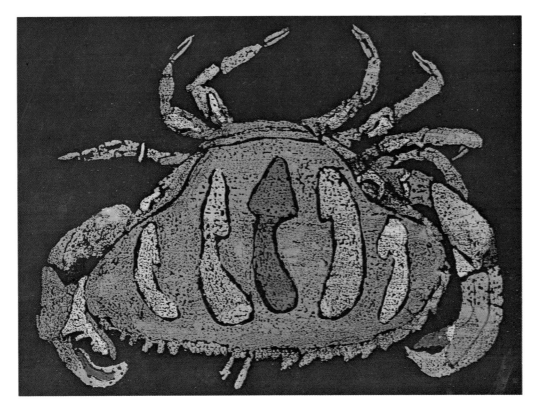

PLATE 33
■ *Sea life oil pastel resist (Lesson 22).*

■ *Tagboard relief print of fantasy creature (Lesson 24).*

PLATE 34

PLATE 35

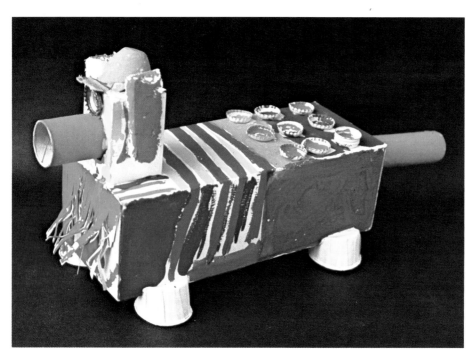

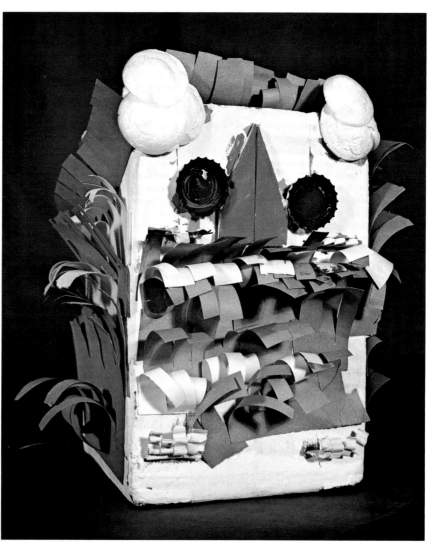

PLATE 36

■ *Fantasy creature box sculpture
(Lesson 27).*

PLATE 37

PLATE 38
■ Clay relief house
(Lesson 28).

PLATE 39
■ Clay relief jungle foliage
(Lesson 29).

PLATE 40
■ *Clay relief fish (Lesson 31).*

PLATE 41
■ *Clay relief animal (Lesson 32).*

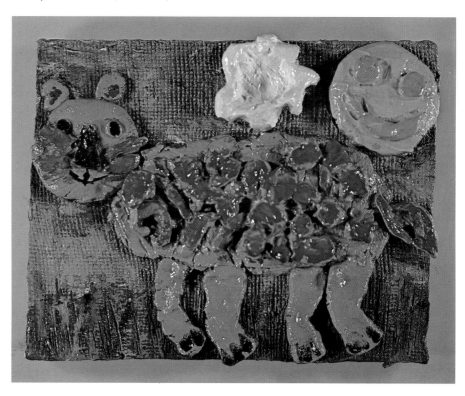

PLATE 42
■ Mood portrait collage
(Lesson 34).

PLATE 43

PLATE 44   ■ *Machine parts tissue paper collage (Lesson 35).*

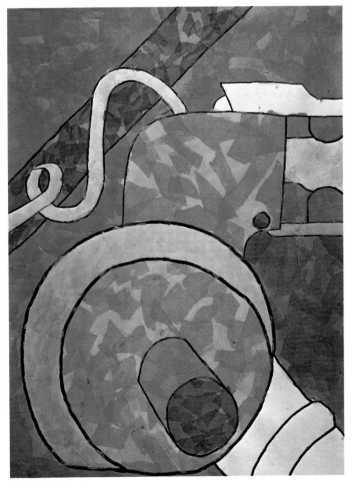

PLATE 45
■ *Machine parts tissue paper collage (Lesson 35).*

PLATE 46
■ *Still life tissue paper collage (Lesson 36).*

PLATE 47

■ Collage mural of our town (Lesson 37).

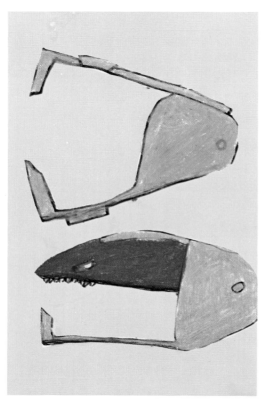

PLATE 48

■ *Metamorphosis marker drawing (Lesson 39).*

PLATE 49

PLATE 50

■ *Oil pastel resist of flower garden (Lesson 40).* **PLATE 51**

■ *Insect crayon engraving (Lesson 41).*

PLATE 52

PLATE 53

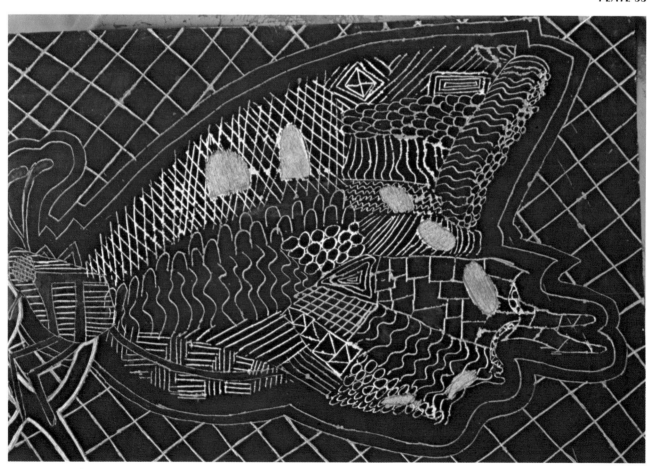

PLATE 54

■ *Experimental landscape painting (Lesson 43).*

PLATE 55

PLATE 56

 Patterned animal relief print (Lesson 44).

PLATE 57

PLATE 58

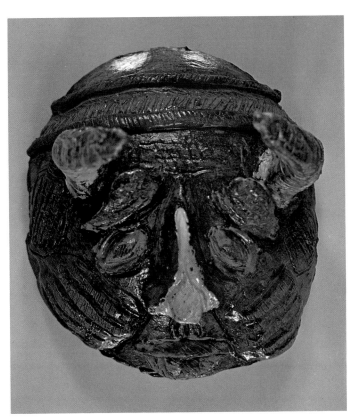

PLATE 59

■ Ceremonial clay mask
(Lesson 46).

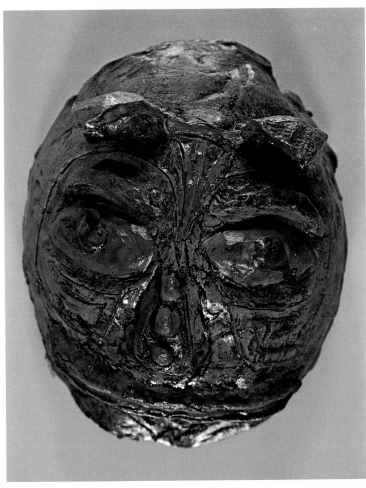

PLATE 60
■ *Life size three-dimensional self-portrait (Lesson 47).*

PLATE 61
■ Effigy pottery (Lesson 51).

PLATE 62
■ Fantasy bird sculpture (Lesson 52).

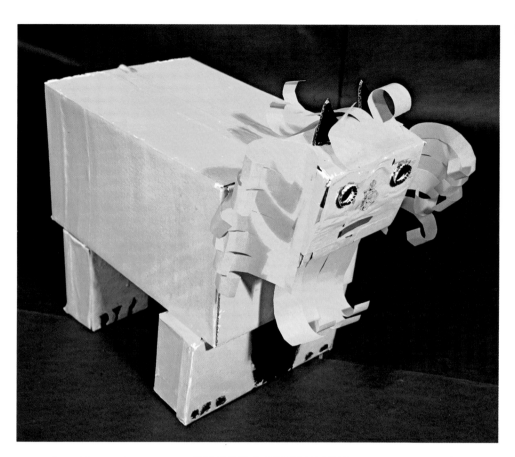

PLATE 63

■ Cardboard box and
construction paper sculpture
(Lesson 53).

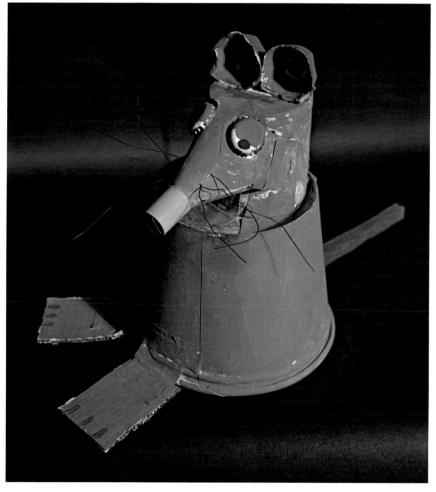

PLATE 64

SUPPLEMENTARY TEACHING AIDS

A. RECOMMENDED MATERIALS
B. TERMS FOR DESCRIBING
   THE ART ELEMENTS
C. VISUAL RESOURCES

RECOMMENDED MATERIALS

Adhesives

white glue
rubber cement
masking tape
wheat paste
epoxy glue (optional)

Brushes

½" pointed brush (#9)
⅛" round (#1)
1" chisel edge bristle brush (#10)

Clay Supplies

water base pre-mixed clay (earthenware)
¼" wood strips
dowel rods and rolling pins
hard plastic knives or fettling knives
forks, spoons
clay modeling tools (optional)
plastic wrap (cleaner bags, bread bags, etc.)
plywood or masonite squares (12")
burlap or canvas (optional)

Cleaning, Maintenance Supplies

newspapers
paper towels
cans of assorted sizes, buckets
sponges
rags
liquid soap
aluminum pie pans
scrub brush

Drawing Materials

pencils (#2)
erasers, school or kneaded
assorted waterproof felt-tip markers, thin and wide
white chalk
crayons
oil pastels
colored pencils
rulers, 12"
permanent black ink

Paints

liquid tempera paints, assorted colors
polymer gloss medium (as protective finish)
wood stain (water base)

Paper

12" × 18" construction paper, assorted colors
12" × 18" white drawing paper
12" × 18" manila paper
12" × 18" newsprint
12" × 18" tissue paper, assorted colors
carbon paper (optional)
tracing paper (optional)
matboard/non-corrugated cardboard (old note pad
    backs)
tagboard (use discarded file folders when smaller
    pieces are needed)
36" wide rolls brown kraft paper (assorted colors
    optional)

Printing Supplies

water-base printing ink, black (other colors
  optional)
brayers, 4″ to 6″
glass or plexiglass inking plates, 9″ × 12″
linoleum cutting tools
linoleum
flexible printing plate (adhesive backing)
  9″ × 12″

Tools, Utensils

scissors
hammer
u-tacks
stapler and staples
wire cutters or pliers
paper punch and reinforcements
compasses
needles and thread
clothespins, paper clips

Miscellaneous

small hand mirrors
magazines (*National Geographic, Smithsonian,
  Vogue, Glamour, National Wildlife*, etc.)
balloons
cotton swabs
fabric scraps, buttons, etc.
wood scraps
sandpaper
boxes, cartons, cardboard
bottle caps
straws
brown paper lunch bags
yarn
string
wire—stovepipe or other flexible yet substantial
  wire

TERMS FOR DESCRIBING THE ART ELEMENTS

Color

advancing—receding
light—dark
opaque—transparent
primary—secondary
saturated—desaturated
warm—cool

Line

continuous—broken
controlled—uncontrolled
curved—straight
hard edge—soft edge
jagged—smooth
open—closed
passive—active
thick—thin

Mass or Volume

additive—subtractive
angular—curved
full—empty
hard—soft
heavy—light
large—small
opaque—transparent
solid—skeletal
stationary—moving

Pattern

ornate—plain
planned—unplanned
progressive—flowing
regular—irregular
repetitious—alternating
symmetrical—nonsymmetrical

Shape or Form

circular—angular
concave—convex
distorted—realistic
dominant—subordinate
functional—nonfunctional
geometric—biomorphic
hard—soft
open—closed
planned—unplanned
positive—negative
precise—vague
proportional—nonproportional
simple—complex
symmetrical—asymmetrical
tall—short
thick—thin
transparent—opaque

Space

balanced—unbalanced
circular—angular
clustered—unclustered
complex—simple
compressive—expansive
dense—sparse
empty—full
flat—deep
linear—nonlinear
ordered—random
overlapping—parallel
positive—negative
spontaneous—deliberate
symmetrical—asymmetrical
three-dimensional—two-dimensional
vertical—horizontal

Texture

artificial—natural
coarse—fine
dull—shiny
raised—lowered
rough—smooth
slippery—dry
soft—hard

VISUAL RESOURCES

Reinhold Publishing Company
600 Summer Street
Stamford, Connecticut 06901

These remarkably attractive and well produced teaching aids provide a wide range of visuals that represent examples of art, design, and the environment. The visuals are organized into 10 portfolios which focus on a particular theme, such as line, mass, color, organization, movement, perception, space, light, fantasy, and illusion. The visuals are 18″ × 24″ in size and each portfolio contains 24 examples.

Sandak, Inc.
180 Harvard Avenue
Stamford, Connecticut 06902

Visual Sources for Learning consists of 28 filmstrips, each containing 20 reproductions of art objects. The filmstrips are organized around four broad themes: (a) Man and Society; (b) Forms from Nature: (c) Man-made World; and (d) Visual themes. The filmstrips are accompanied by a guide which helps the teacher to focus on major issues within each series. The reproductions are expertly selected and provide teachers and students with a sensitive treatment of each of these themes.

Society for Visual Education, Inc.
1345 W. Diversey Parkway
Chicago, Illinois 60614

The Society has a collection of filmstrips and picture story study prints representing an extraordinary range of social, anthropological, scientific, environmental, zoological, seasonal, and geographic topics. These visuals are particularly helpful in stimulating a child's thought processes and concretely demonstrating the range and variation of a particular topic.

Art Works

Visuals representing exemplary works of famous artists can be purchased through any regional art and educational materials dealer. The visuals should be on heavy paper stock and be suitable for general classroom display. It is important that the visuals purchased be representative of major artistic styles and subject matter, in order that students may have the opportunity to review the multiplicity of solutions to artistic problems.

BIBLIOGRAPHY

ART AND EDUCATION

THE ARTS, EDUCATION AND AMERICANS PANEL. *Coming to Our Senses: The Significance of the Arts for American Education.* New York: McGraw-Hill, 1977.

BARZUN, J. "Art and Educational Inflation." *Art Education,* 1978, *31*(7), 4–10.

BROUDY, H. S. *Arts Education as Artistic Perception.* Address, Conference on the Foundations of Education, Lehigh University, March 28, 1974.

—. "How Basic Is Aesthetic Education? or Is 'Rt the Fourth R?" *Language Arts,* 1977, *54*(6), 631–637.

DORN, C. M. "The New Eclecticism, or Art Is Anything You Can Get Away With." *Art Education,* 1978, *31*(8), 6–9.

EISNER, E. W. "The State of Art Education Today and Some Potential Remedies." A report to the National Endowment for the Arts. *Art Education,* 1978, *31*(8), 14–23.

FELDMAN, E. B. "Catalyst—the Arts." *Art Education,* 1978, *31*(7), 6–11.

FOSHAY, A. W. "The Arts in General Education." *Art Education,* 1973, *26*(6), 2–6.

LANGER, S. "The Cultural Importance of the Arts." In M. F. Andrews (Ed.), *Aesthetic Form and Education.* Syracuse, N.Y.: Syracuse University Press, 1958.

NATIONAL RESEARCH CENTER OF THE ARTS, Inc. *Arts and the People.* New York: Publishing Center for Cultural Resources, 1973.

RUSSELL, J. E. "The Role of Arts in Education." *Conference on Curriculum and Instruction Development in Art Education: A Project Report.* Washington, D.C.: National Art Education Association, 1967.

PSYCHOLOGICAL STUDIES

ARNHEIM, R. *Art and Visual Perception.* Berkeley, Calif.: University of California Press, 1954.

BRAINE, M. D. S. "The Ontogeny of Certain Logical Operations: Piaget's Formulation Examined by Nonverbal Methods." *Psychological Monographs,* 1969, *73*(5, Whole No. 475).

CHAPMAN, L. H. *Approaches to Art in Education.* New York: Harcourt Brace Jovanovich, 1978.

DeVRIES, R. *Evaluation of Cognitive Development with Piaget-type Tests: A Study of Young, Bright, Average, and Retarded Children.* Urbana, Ill.: ERIC Document Reproduction Service No. ECE 075 065, 1971.

DUDEK, S. Z.; LESTER, E. P.; and others. "Relationship of Piaget Measures to Standard Intelligence and Motor Scales." *Perceptual and Motor Skills, 1969, 28,* 351–362.

EISNER, E. W. (Ed.). *The Arts, Human Development, and Education.* Berkeley, Calif.: McCutchan, 1976.

ELKIND, D. "The Development of Quantitative Thinking." *Journal of Genetic Psychology,* 1961, *98,* 36–46.

FELDMAN, E. B. *Becoming Human Through Art.* Englewood Cliffs, N.J.: Prentice-Hall, 1970.

FLAVELL, J. H. *The Developmental Psychology of Jean Piaget.* Princeton, N.J.: Van Nostrand, 1963.

—. "Concept Development." In P. H. Mussen (Ed.), *Carmichael's Manual of Child Psychology* (Vol. 1). New York: Wiley, 1970.

—. "Stage-related Properties of Cognitive Development." *Cognitive Psychology,* 1971, *2,* 421–453.

FLAVELL J. H., and WOHLWILL, J. F. "Formal and Functional Aspects of Cognitive Development." In D. Elkind and J. H. Flavell (Eds.), *Studies in Cognitive Development: Essays in Honor of Jean Piaget.* New York: Oxford University Press, 1969.

FREYBERG, P. S. "Concept Development in Piagetian Terms in Relation to School Attainment." *Journal of Educational Psychology,* 1966, *57*(3), 164–168.

FURTH, H. G. *Piaget and Knowledge: Theoretical Foundations.* Englewood Cliffs, N.J.: Prentice-Hall, 1969.

GAGNÉ, R. M. "Contributions of Learning to Human Development." *Psychological Review,* 1968, *75,* 177–191.

GAITSKELL, C. D., and HURWITZ, A. *Children and Their Art* (3rd ed.). New York: Harcourt Brace Jovanovich, 1975.

GARDNER, H. *Child Development: An Introduction.* Boston: Little, Brown, 1977.

GOLOMB, C. *Young Children's Sculpture and Drawing.* Cambridge, Mass.: Harvard University Press, 1974.

GOODENOUGH, F. L. "The Measurement of Mental Growth in Childhood." In L. Carmichael (Ed.), *Manual of Child Psychology* (2nd ed.). New York: Wiley, 1954.

GOODNOW, J. *Children Drawing.* Cambridge, Mass.: Harvard University Press, 1977.

HARDIMAN, G. W. and ZERNICH, T. "Influence of Style and Subject Matter on the Development of Children's Art Preferences." *Studies in Art Education,* 1977, *19:1,* 29–35.

KELLOGG, R. *What Children Scribble and Why.* San Francisco: N-P Publications, 1959.

KLAHR, D., and WALLACE, J. G. "An Information Processing Analysis of Some Piagetian Experimental Tasks. *Cognitive Psychology,* 1970, *1,* 358–387.

KOHLBERG, L. "Stage and Sequence: The Cognitive-developmental Approach to Socialization." In D. A. Goslin (Ed.), *Handbook of Socialization Theory and Research.* San Francisco: Rand McNally, 1969.

KOHLBERG, L., and MAYER, R. "Development as the Aim of Education." *Harvard Educational Review,* 1973, *42*(4), 449–496.

LARK-HOROVITZ, B.; LEWIS, H. P.; and LUCA, M. *Understanding Children's Art for Better Teaching.* Columbus, Ohio: Charles E. Merrill, 1967.

LOWENFELD, V. *Creative and Mental Growth* (3rd ed.). New York: MacMillan, 1957.

MISCHEL, T. "Piaget, Cognitive Conflict and the Motivation of Thought. In T. Mischel (Ed.), *Cognitive Development and Epistemology.* New York: Academic Press, 1971.

PIAGET, J. *The Language and Thought of the Child.* New York: Harcourt Brace, 1926.

—. *Judgment and Reasoning in the Child.* New York: Harcourt, Brace, 1928.

—. *The Origins of Intelligence in Children.* New York: International Universities Presss, 1952.

—. "The Mechanisms of Perception. (G.N. Seagrim, trans.) New York: Basic Books, 1969.

PIAGET, J., and INHELDER, B. *The Child's Conception of Space.* London: Routledge & Kegan Paul, 1956.

PINARD, A., and LAURENDEAU, M. "*Stage* in Piaget's Cognitive-developmental Theory: Exegesis of a Concept." In D. Elkind and J. H. Flavell (Eds.), *Studies in Cognitive Development.* New York: Oxford University Press, 1969.

REST, J., TURIEL, E., and KOHLBERG, L. "Relations between Level of Moral Judgment and Preference and Comprehension of the Moral Judgment of Others." *Journal of Personality,* 1969, *37,* 225–252.

SMEDSLUND, J. "Concrete Reasoning: A Study of Intellectual Development." *Society for Research in Child Development Monographs,* 1964, *29*(2, Serial No. 93).

WERNER, H. "The Concept of Development from a Comparative and Organismic Point of View." In D. B. Harris (Ed.), *The Concept of Development,* Minneapolis: University of Minnesota Press, 1957.

WOHLWILL, J. F. "Piaget's System as a Source of Empirical Research." *Merrill-Palmer Quarterly,* 1963, *9,* 253–262.

—. "The Age Variable in Psychological Research." *Psychological Review,* 1970, *77,* 49–64.

—. "Methodology and Research Strategy in the Study of Developmental Change." In L. R. Goulet and P. B. Baltes (Eds.), *Theory and Research in Life-span Developmental Psychology.* New York: Academic Press, 1970.

ABOUT THE AUTHOR

Dr. Mary Alice Jones is one of this country's recognized authorities on religious education for children and is the author of many best-selling children's books in the field of religion. She has prepared this book especially to help parents with their important task of bringing young children to know the Baby Jesus.

First printing, 1964
Second printing, 1964
Third printing, 1965
Fourth printing, 1965
Fifth printing, 1966

The Baby
JESUS

By Mary Alice Jones

Illustrated by Elizabeth Webbe

 RAND McNALLY & COMPANY · Chicago

Established 1856

Copyright © MCMLXI by Rand McNally & Company. Copyright MCMLXI under International Copyright Union by Rand McNally & Company. All rights reserved. Printed in U.S.A. Library of Congress Catalog Card Number: 64–15251.

Bible text used: LUKE 2:4-8; 1:31b

Mary and Joseph were going to Bethlehem. Mary was riding on a little gray donkey. Joseph was walking, leading the donkey.

Mary and Joseph went on and on.
The sun went down. It was getting
cold. As Mary and Joseph passed a

field they saw the sheep coming close
together to keep warm. They saw
shepherds making a fire.

Soon it would be dark. Mary
was tired. She knew it was time for
her baby to be born. She drew her
shawl closer about her to keep warm.

"There," Joseph said. "There is Bethlehem. It is not far now."

Mary looked up and saw the town. "We are almost there," she said.

Mary and Joseph came to the town. They went to the inn where travelers stayed. The door was closed.

Joseph knocked at the door. He
knocked again and again.

The inn keeper opened the door. He held up his lantern. When he saw that a traveler was there he shook his head. "We have no room left," he said. "The inn is full."

"But what can we do?" Joseph asked. "Mary is very tired. She will

soon have a baby. I must find a place
where Mary can be warm and rest."

The inn keeper sighed. "I want to help you," he said. "But so many people have come tonight. There is a stable back of the inn where we keep the cow. It is warm. There is straw for a bed. There is no other place. I will lend you a lantern."

Joseph wanted a nicer place for Mary. But Mary smiled. "It is all right, Joseph," she said. "We will be warm in the stable. We can have a straw bed."

So Joseph led the donkey to the stable. And Mary got-off the donkey and went into the stable.

Joseph hung the lantern on a peg. He made a straw bed for Mary. He put his long cloak over her. As Mary rested, Joseph fed the donkey.

Mary was warm in the stable. The donkey and the cow were warm.

Outside it was cold. The little town
of Bethlehem was quiet. Everyone was
in bed.

Everybody was asleep. Then Mary woke up. Joseph woke up. Mary knew that soon she would have her baby. And before daylight came, the baby

was born. Mary wrapped the tiny
baby in the soft clothes she had
brought.

Joseph said, "He is the loveliest
baby in all the world, Mary."

Joseph went to the door. He saw
stars and stars and stars in the sky.
They had never seemed so bright. Far
away he seemed to hear happy voices

singing. Joseph turned to look at Mary and the baby. "Even the skies seem to be happy tonight, Mary. The skies seem to be glad about your baby."

Mary held the baby close. No one, not even Joseph, could know how happy she was. "His name will be Jesus," she said.

Joseph said, "His name will be Jesus."

And Mary sang a little song to the baby Jesus. And outside, the bright stars shone and the happy voices sang.